Helen Keller in Her Study

The World I Live In
and
Optimism

A Collection of Essays

HELEN KELLER

DOVER PUBLICATIONS, INC.
Mineola, New York

Bibliographical Note

This Dover edition, first published in 2009, contains the unabridged texts of *The World I Live In*, originally published by The Century Company, New York, in 1908, and *Optimism, An Essay*, originally published by T. Y. Crowell and Company, New York, in 1903.

Library of Congress Cataloging-in-Publication Data

Keller, Helen, 1880–1968.
    The world I live in and Optimism: a collection of essays / Helen Keller.
        p. cm.
    "This Dover edition, first published in 2009, contains the unabridged texts of The World I Live In, originally published by The Century Company, New York, in 1908, and Optimism, An Essay, originally published by T. Y. Crowell and Company, New York, in 1903."
    ISBN-13: 978-0-486-47367-3
    ISBN-10: 0-486-47367-8
        1. Senses and sensation.   2. Perception.   3. Keller, Helen, 1880–1968.
4. Optimism.   I. Keller, Helen, 1880–1968. My key of life, optimism.   II. Title.
HV1624.K4A3 2009
362.4'1092—dc22
[B]

2009024684

Manufactured in the United States by LSC Communications
47367807   2018
www.doverpublications.com

CONTENTS

Optimism

ILLUSTRATIONS

THE WORLD I LIVE IN

PREFACE

The essays and the poem in this book appeared originally in the "Century Magazine," the essays under the titles "A Chat About the Hand," "Sense and Sensibility," and "My Dreams." Mr. Gilder suggested the articles, and I thank him for his kind interest and encouragement. But he must also accept the responsibility which goes with my gratitude. For it is owing to his wish and that of other editors that I talk so much about myself.

Every book is in a sense autobiographical. But while other self-recording creatures are permitted at least to seem to change the subject, apparently nobody cares what I think of the tariff, the conservation of our natural resources, or the conflicts which revolve about the name of Dreyfus. If I offer to reform the educational system of the world, my editorial friends say, "That is interesting. But will you please tell us what idea you had of goodness and beauty when you were six years old?" First they ask me to tell the life of the child who is mother to the woman. Then they make me my own daughter and ask for an account of grown-up sensations. Finally I am requested to write about my dreams, and thus I become an anachronical grandmother; for it is the special privilege of old age to relate dreams. The editors are so kind that they are no doubt right in thinking that nothing I have to say about the affairs of the universe would be interesting. But until they give me opportunity to write about matters that are not-me, the world must go on uninstructed and unreformed, and I can only do my best with the one small subject upon which I am allowed to discourse.

xii PREFACE

In "The Chant of Darkness" I did not intend to set up as a poet. I thought I was writing prose, except for the magnificent passage from Job which I was paraphrasing. But this part seemed to my friends to separate itself from the exposition, and I made it into a kind of poem.

H. K.

Wrentham, Massachusetts,
July 1st, 1908.

I. The Seeing Hand

I HAVE just touched my dog. He was rolling on the grass, with pleasure in every muscle and limb. I wanted to catch a picture of him in my fingers, and I touched him as lightly as I would cobwebs; but lo, his fat body revolved, stiffened and solidified into an upright position, and his tongue gave my hand a lick! He pressed close to me, as if he were fain to crowd himself into my hand. He loved it with his tail, with his paw, with his tongue. If he could speak, I believe he would say with me that paradise is attained by touch; for in touch is all love and intelligence.

This small incident started me on a chat about hands, and if my chat is fortunate I have to thank my dog-star. In any case, it is pleasant to have something to talk about that no one else has monopolized; it is like making a new path in the trackless woods, blazing the trail where no foot has pressed before. I am glad to take you by the hand and lead you along an untrodden way into a world where the hand is supreme. But at the very outset we encounter a difficulty. You are so accustomed to light, I fear you will stumble when I try to guide you through the land of darkness and silence. The blind are not supposed to be the best of guides. Still, though I cannot warrant not to lose you, I promise that you shall not be led into fire or water, or fall into a deep pit. If you will follow me patiently, you will find that "there's a sound so fine, nothing lives 'twixt it and silence," and that there is more meant in things than meets the eye.

My hand is to me what your hearing and sight together are to you. In large measure we travel the same highways, read the same books, speak the same language, yet our experiences are

1

different. All my comings and goings turn on the hand as on a pivot. It is the hand that binds me to the world of men and women. The hand is my feeler with which I reach through isolation and darkness and seize every pleasure, every activity that my fingers encounter. With the dropping of a little word from another's hand into mine, a slight flutter of the fingers, began the intelligence, the joy, the fullness of my life. Like Job, I feel as if a hand had made me, fashioned me together round about and molded my very soul.

In all my experiences and thoughts I am conscious of a hand. Whatever moves me, whatever thrills me, is as a hand that touches me in the dark, and that touch is my reality. You might as well say that a sight which makes you glad, or a blow which brings the stinging tears to your eyes, is unreal as to say that those impressions are unreal which I have accumulated by means of touch. The delicate tremble of a butterfly's wings in my hand, the soft petals of violets curling in the cool folds of their leaves or lifting sweetly out of the meadow-grass, the clear, firm outline of face and limb, the smooth arch of a horse's neck and the velvety touch of his nose—all these, and a thousand resultant combinations, which take shape in my mind, constitute my world.

Ideas make the world we live in, and impressions furnish ideas. My world is built of touch-sensations, devoid of physical color and sound; but without color and sound it breathes and throbs with life. Every object is associated in my mind with tactual qualities which, combined in countless ways, give me a sense of power, of beauty, or of incongruity: for with my hands I can feel the comic as well as the beautiful in the outward appearance of things. Remember that you, dependent on your sight, do not realize how many things are tangible. All palpable things are mobile or rigid, solid or liquid, big or small, warm or cold, and these qualities are variously modified. The coolness of a water-lily rounding into bloom is different from the coolness of an evening wind in summer, and different again from the coolness of the rain that soaks into the hearts of growing things and gives them life and body. The velvet of the rose is not that of a ripe peach or of a baby's dimpled cheek. The hardness of the rock is to the hardness of wood what a man's deep bass is to a woman's voice when it is low. What I call beauty I find in certain combinations of all these qualities, and is largely derived from the flow of curved and straight lines which is over all things.

"What does the straight line mean to you?" I think you will ask.

It *means* several things. It symbolizes duty. It seems to have the quality of inexorableness that duty has. When I have something to do that must not be set aside, I feel as if I were going forward in a straight line, bound to arrive somewhere, or go on forever without swerving to the right or to the left.

That is what it means. To escape this moralizing you should ask, "How does the straight line feel?" It feels, as I suppose it looks, straight—a dull thought drawn out endlessly. Eloquence to the touch resides not in straight lines, but in unstraight lines, or in many curved and straight lines together. They appear and disappear, are now deep, now shallow, now broken off or lengthened or swelling. They rise and sink beneath my fingers, they are full of sudden starts and pauses, and their variety is inexhaustible and wonderful. So you see I am not shut out from the region of the beautiful, though my hand cannot perceive the brilliant colors in the sunset or on the mountain, or reach into the blue depths of the sky.

Physics tells me that I am well off in a world which, I am told, knows neither color nor sound, but is made in terms of size, shape, and inherent qualities; for at least every object appears to my fingers standing solidly right side up, and is not an inverted image on the retina which, I understand, your brain is at infinite though unconscious labor to set back on its feet. A tangible object passes complete into my brain with the warmth of life upon it, and occupies the same place that it does in space; for, without egotism, the mind is as large as the universe. When I think of hills, I think of the upward strength I tread upon. When water is the object of my thought, I feel the cool shock of the plunge and the quick yielding of the waves that crisp and curl and ripple about my body. The pleasing changes of rough and smooth, pliant and rigid, curved and straight in the bark and branches of a tree give the truth to my hand. The immovable rock, with its juts and warped surface, bends beneath my fingers into all manner of grooves and hollows. The bulge of a watermelon and the puffed-up rotundities of squashes that sprout, bud, and ripen in that strange garden planted somewhere behind my finger-tips are the ludicrous in my tactual memory and imagination. My fingers are tickled to delight by the soft ripple of a baby's laugh, and find amusement in the lusty crow of the barnyard autocrat. Once I had a pet rooster that used to perch on my knee and stretch his neck and crow. A bird in my hand was then worth two in the—barnyard.

My fingers cannot, of course, get the impression of a large whole at a glance; but I feel the parts, and my mind puts them together. I move around my house, touching object after object in order, before I can form an idea of the entire house. In other people's houses I can touch only what is shown me—the chief objects of interest, carvings on the wall, or a curious architectural feature, exhibited like the family album. Therefore a house with which I am not familiar has for me, at first, no general effect or harmony of detail. It is not a complete conception, but a collection of object-impressions which, as they come to me, are disconnected and isolated. But my mind is full of associations, sensations, theories, and with them it constructs the house. The process reminds me of the building of Solomon's temple, where was neither saw, nor hammer, nor any tool heard while the stones were being laid one upon another. The silent worker is imagination which decrees reality out of chaos.

Without imagination what a poor thing my world would be! My garden would be a silent patch of earth strewn with sticks of a variety of shapes and smells. But when the eye of my mind is opened to its beauty, the bare ground brightens beneath my feet, and the hedge-row bursts into leaf, and the rose-tree shakes its fragrance everywhere. I know how budding trees look, and I enter into the amorous joy of the mating birds, and this is the miracle of imagination.

Twofold is the miracle when, through my fingers, my imagination reaches forth and meets the imagination of an artist which he has embodied in a sculptured form. Although, compared with the life-warm, mobile face of a friend, the marble is cold and pulseless and unresponsive, yet it is beautiful to my hand. Its flowing curves and bendings are a real pleasure; only breath is wanting; but under the spell of the imagination the marble thrills and becomes the divine reality of the ideal. Imagination puts a sentiment into every line and curve, and the statue in my touch is indeed the goddess herself who breathes and moves and enchants.

It is true, however, that some sculptures, even recognized masterpieces, do not please my hand. When I touch what there is of the Winged Victory, it reminds me at first of a headless, limbless dream that flies towards me in an unrestful sleep. The garments of the Victory thrust stiffly out behind, and do not resemble garments that I have felt flying, fluttering, folding, spreading in the wind. But imagination fulfils these imperfections, and straightway the Victory becomes a powerful and spirited figure with the sweep of sea-winds in her robes and the splendor of conquest in her wings.

I find in a beautiful statue perfection of bodily form, the qualities of balance and completeness. The Minerva, hung with a web of poetical allusion, gives me a sense of exhilaration that is almost physical; and I like the luxuriant, wavy hair of Bacchus and Apollo, and the wreath of ivy, so suggestive of pagan holidays.

So imagination crowns the experience of my hands. And they learned their cunning from the wise hand of another, which, itself guided by imagination, led me safely in paths that I knew not, made darkness light before me, and made crooked ways straight.

II. The Hands of Others

THE warmth and protectiveness of the hand are most homefelt to me who have always looked to it for aid and joy. I understand perfectly how the Psalmist can lift up his voice with strength and gladness, singing, "I put my trust in the Lord at all times, and his hand shall uphold me, and I shall dwell in safety." In the strength of the human hand, too, there is something divine. I am told that the glance of a beloved eye thrills one from a distance; but there is no distance in the touch of a beloved hand. Even the letters I receive are—

> Kind letters that betray the heart's deep history,
> In which we feel the presence of a hand.

It is interesting to observe the differences in the hands of people. They show all kinds of vitality, energy, stillness, and cordiality. I never realized how living the hand is until I saw those chill plaster images in Mr. Hutton's collection of casts. The hand I know in life has the fullness of blood in its veins, and is elastic with spirit. How different dear Mr. Hutton's hand was from its dull, insensate image! To me the cast lacks the very form of the hand. Of the many casts in Mr. Hutton's collection I did not recognize any, not even my own. But a loving hand I never forget. I remember in my fingers the large hands of Bishop Brooks, brimful of tenderness and a strong man's joy. If you were deaf and blind, and could have held Mr. Jefferson's hand, you would have seen in it a face and heard a kind voice unlike any other you have known. Mark Twain's hand is full of whimsies and the drollest humors, and while you hold it the drollery changes to sympathy and championship.

I am told that the words I have just written do not "describe" the hands of my friends, but merely endow them with the kindly human qualities which I know they possess, and which language conveys in abstract words. The criticism implies that I am not giving the primary truth of what I feel; but how otherwise do descriptions in books I read, written by men who can see, render the visible look of a face? I read that a face is strong, gentle; that it is full of patience, of intellect; that it is fine, sweet, noble, beautiful. Have I not the same right to use these words in describing what I feel as you have in describing what you see? They express truly what I feel in the hand. I am seldom conscious of physical qualities, and I do not remember whether the fingers of a hand are short or long, or the skin is moist or dry. No more can you, without conscious effort, recall the details of a face, even when you have seen it many times. If you do recall the features, and say that an eye is blue, a chin sharp, a nose short, or a cheek sunken, I fancy that you do not succeed well in giving the impression of the person,—not so well as when you interpret at once to the heart the essential moral qualities of the face—its humor, gravity, sadness, spirituality. If I should tell you in physical terms how a hand feels, you would be no wiser for my account than a blind man to whom you describe a face in detail. Remember that when a blind man recovers his sight, he does not recognize the commonest thing that has been familiar to his touch, the dearest face intimate to his fingers, and it does not help him at all that things and people have been described to him again and again. So you, who are untrained of touch, do not recognize a hand by the grasp; and so, too, any description I might give would fail to make you acquainted with a friendly hand which my fingers have often folded about, and which my affection translates to my memory.

I cannot describe hands under any class or type; there is no democracy of hands. Some hands tell me that they do everything with the maximum of bustle and noise. Other hands are fidgety and unadvised, with nervous, fussy fingers which indicate a nature sensitive to the little pricks of daily life. Some-times I recognize with foreboding the kindly but stupid hand of one who tells with many words news that is no news. I have met a bishop with a jocose hand, a humorist with a hand of leaden gravity, a man of pretentious valor with a timorous hand, and a quiet, apologetic man with a fist of iron. When I was a little girl I was taken to see[1] a woman who was blind and paralyzed. I shall never forget how she held out her small, trembling hand and pressed sympathy into mine. My eyes fill with tears as I think of her. The weariness, pain, darkness, and sweet patience were all to be felt in her thin, wasted, groping, loving hand.

Few people who do not know me will understand, I think, how much I get of the mood of a friend who is engaged in oral conversation with somebody else. My hand follows his motions; I touch his hand, his arm, his face. I can tell when he is full of glee over a good joke which has not been repeated to me, or when he is telling a lively story. One of my friends is rather aggressive, and his hand always announces the coming of a dispute. By his impatient jerk I know he has argument ready for some one. I have felt him start as a sudden recollection or a new idea shot through his mind. I have felt grief in his hand. I have felt his soul wrap itself in darkness majestically as in a garment. Another friend has positive, emphatic hands which show great pertinac-ity of opinion. She is the only person I know who emphasizes her spelled words and accents them as she emphasizes and accents her spoken words when I read her lips. I like this varied emphasis better than the monotonous pound of unmodulated people who hammer their meaning into my palm.

Some hands, when they clasp yours, beam and bubble over with gladness. They throb and expand with life. Strangers have clasped my hand like that of a long-lost sister. Other people shake hands with me as if with the fear that I may do them

---

[1] The excellent proof-reader has put a query to my use of the word "see." If I had said "visit," he would have asked no questions, yet what does "visit" mean but "see" (*visitare*)? Later I will try to defend myself for using as much of the English language as I have succeeded in learning.

mischief. Such persons hold out civil finger-tips which they permit you to touch, and in the moment of contract they retreat, and inwardly you hope that you will not be called upon again to take that hand of "dormouse valor." It betokens a prudish mind, ungracious pride, and not seldom mistrust. It is the antipode to the hand of those who have large, lovable natures.

The handshake of some people makes you think of accident and sudden death. Contrast this ill-boding hand with the quick, skilful, quiet hand of a nurse whom I remember with affection because she took the best care of my teacher. I have clasped the hands of some rich people that spin not and toil not, and yet are not beautiful. Beneath their soft, smooth roundness what a chaos of undeveloped character!

I am sure there is no hand comparable to the physician's in patient skill, merciful gentleness and splendid certainty. No wonder that Ruskin finds in the sure strokes of the surgeon the perfection of control and delicate precision for the artist to emulate. If the physician is a man of great nature, there will be healing for the spirit in his touch. This magic touch of well-being was in the hand of a dear friend of mine who was our doctor in sickness and health. His happy cordial spirit did his patients good whether they needed medicine or not.

As there are many beauties of the face, so the beauties of the hand are many. Touch has its ecstasies. The hands of people of strong individuality and sensitiveness are wonderfully mobile. In a glance of their finger-tips they express many shades of thought. Now and again I touch a fine, graceful, supple-wristed hand which spells with the same beauty and distinction that you must see in the handwriting of some highly cultivated people. I wish you could see how prettily little children spell in my hand. They are wild flowers of humanity, and their finger motions wild flowers of speech.

All this is my private science of palmistry, and when I tell your fortune it is by no mysterious intuition or Gipsy witchcraft, but by natural, explicable recognition of the embossed character in your hand. Not only is the hand as easy to recognize as the face, but it reveals its secrets more openly and unconsciously.

People control their countenances, but the hand is under no such restraint. It relaxes and becomes listless when the spirit is low and dejected; the muscles tighten when the mind is excited or the heart glad; and permanent qualities stand written on it all the time.

III. The Hand of the Race

Look in your "Century Dictionary," or if you are blind, ask your teacher to do it for you, and learn how many idioms are made on the idea of hand, and how many words are formed from the Latin root *manus*—enough words to name all the essential affairs of life. "Hand," with quotations and compounds, occupies twenty-four columns, eight pages of this dictionary. The hand is defined as "the organ of apprehension." How perfectly the definition fits my case in both senses of the word "apprehend"! With my hand I seize and hold all that I find in the three worlds—physical, intellectual, and spiritual.

Think how man has regarded the world in terms of the hand. All life is divided between what lies *on one hand* and on the other. The products of skill are *manu*factures. The conduct of affairs is *man*agement. History seems to be the record—alas for our chronicles of war!—of the *manœuvres* of armies. But the history of peace, too, the narrative of labor in the field, the forest, and the vineyard, is written in the victorious sign *manual*— the sign of the hand that has conquered the wilderness. The laborer himself is called a *hand*. In *man*acle and *manu*mission we read the story of human slavery and freedom.

The minor idioms are myriad; but I will not recall too many, lest you cry, "Hands off!" I cannot desist, however, from this word-game until I have set down a few. Whatever is not one's own by first possession is *second-hand*. That is what I am told my knowledge is. But my well-meaning friends come to my defense, and, not content with endowing me with natural *first-hand* knowledge which is rightfully mine, ascribe to me a preternatural sixth sense and credit to miracles and heaven-sent compensations all that I have won and discovered with my good right hand. And with my left hand too; for with that I read, and it is as true and honorable as the other. By what half-development of human power has the left hand been neglected? When we arrive at the acme of civilization shall we not all be ambidextrous, and in our *hand-to-hand* contests against difficulties shall we not be doubly triumphant? It occurs to me, by the way, that when my teacher was training my unreclaimed spirit, her struggle against the powers of darkness, with the stout arm of discipline and the light of the manual alphabet, was in two senses a hand-to-hand conflict.

No essay would be complete without quotations from Shakespeare. In the field which, in the presumption of my youth, I thought was my own he has reaped before me. In almost every play there are passages where the hand plays a part. Lady Macbeth's heartbroken soliloquy over her little hand, from which all the perfumes of Arabia will not wash the stain, is the most pitiful moment in the tragedy. Mark Antony rewards Scarus, the bravest of his soldiers, by asking Cleopatra to give him her hand: "Commend unto his lips thy favoring hand." In a different mood he is enraged because Thyreus, whom he despises, has presumed to kiss the hand of the queen, "my playfellow, the kingly seal of high hearts." When Cleopatra is threatened with the humiliation of gracing Cæsar's triumph, she snatches a dagger, exclaiming, "I will trust my resolution and my good hands." With the same swift instinct, Cassius trusts to his hands when he stabs Cæsar: "Speak, hands, for me!" "Let me kiss your hand," says the blind Gloster to Lear. "Let me wipe it first," replies the broken old king; "it smells of mortality." How charged is this single touch with sad meaning! How it opens our eyes to the fearful purging Lear has undergone, to learn that royalty is no defense against ingratitude and cruelty! Gloster's exclamation about his son, "Did I but live to see thee in my touch, I'd say I had eyes again," is as true to a pulse within me as the grief he feels. The ghost in "Hamlet" recites the wrongs from which springs the tragedy:

> Thus was I, sleeping, by a brother's hand.
> At once of life, of crown, of queen dispatch'd.

How that passage in "Othello" stops your breath—that passage full of bitter double intention in which Othello's suspicion tips with evil what he says about Desdemona's hand; and she in innocence answers only the innocent meaning of his words: "For 't was that hand that gave away my heart."

Not all Shakespeare's great passages about the hand are tragic. Remember the light play of words in "Romeo and Juliet" where the dialogue, flying nimbly back and forth, weaves a pretty sonnet about the hand. And who knows the hand, if not the lover?

The touch of the hand is in every chapter of the Bible. Why, you could almost rewrite Exodus as the story of the hand. Everything is done by the hand of the Lord and of Moses. The oppression of the Hebrews is translated thus: "The hand of Pharaoh was heavy upon the Hebrews." Their departure out of the land is told in these vivid words: "The Lord brought the children of Israel out of the house of bondage with a strong hand and a stretched-out arm." At the stretching out of the hand of Moses the waters of the Red Sea part and stand all on a heap. When the Lord lifts his hand in anger, thousands perish in the wilderness. Every act, every decree in the history of Israel, as indeed in the history of the human race, is sanctioned by the hand. Is it not used in the great moments of swearing, blessing, cursing, smiting, agreeing, marrying, building, destroying? Its sacredness is in the law that no sacrifice is valid unless the sacrificer lay his hand upon the head of the victim. The congregation lay their hands on the heads of those who are sentenced to death. How terrible the dumb condemnation of their hands must be to the condemned! When Moses builds the altar on Mount Sinai, he is commanded to use no tool, but rear it with his own hands. Earth, sea, sky, man, and all lower animals are holy unto the Lord because he has formed them with his hand. When the Psalmist considers the heavens and the earth, he exclaims: "What is man, O Lord, that thou art mindful of him? For thou hast made him to have dominion over the works of thy hands." The supplicating gesture of the hand always accompanies the spoken prayer, and with clean hands goes the pure heart.

Christ comforted and blessed and healed and wrought many

miracles with his hands. He touched the eyes of the blind, and they were opened. When Jairus sought him, overwhelmed with grief, Jesus went and laid his hands on the ruler's daughter, and she awoke from the sleep of death to her father's love. You also remember how he healed the crooked woman. He said to her, "Woman, thou art loosed from thine infirmity," and he laid his hands on her, and immediately she was made straight, and she glorified God.

Look where we will, we find the hand in time and history, working, building, inventing, bringing civilization out of barbarism. The hand symbolizes power and the excellence of work. The mechanic's hand, that minister of elemental forces, the hand that hews, saws, cuts, builds, is useful in the world equally with the delicate hand that paints a wild flower or molds a Grecian urn, or the hand of a statesman that writes a law. The eye cannot say to the hand, "I have no need of thee." Blessed be the hand! Thrice blessed be the hands that work!

IV. The Power of Touch

S OME months ago, in a newspaper which announced the pub-
lication of the "Matilda Ziegler Magazine for the Blind,"
appeared the following paragraph:

"Many poems and stories must be omitted because they deal
with sight. Allusion to moonbeams, rainbows, starlight, clouds,
and beautiful scenery may not be printed, because they serve to
emphasize the blind man's sense of his affliction."

That is to say, I may not talk about beautiful mansions and
gardens because I am poor. I may not read about Paris and the
West Indies because I cannot visit them in their territorial reality. I may not dream of heaven because it is possible that I may
never go there. Yet a venturesome spirit impels me to use words
of sight and sound whose meaning I can guess only from analogy
and fancy. This hazardous game is half the delight, the frolic, of
daily life. I glow as I read of splendors which the eye alone can
survey. Allusions to moonbeams and clouds do not emphasize
the sense of my affliction: they carry my soul beyond affliction's
narrow actuality.

Critics delight to tell us what we cannot do. They assume
that blindness and deafness sever us completely from the things
which the seeing and the hearing enjoy, and hence they assert
we have no moral right to talk about beauty, the skies, mountains, the song of birds, and colors. They declare that the very
sensations we have from the sense of touch are "vicarious,"
as though our friends felt the sun for us! They deny *a priori*
what they have not seen and I have felt. Some brave doubters have gone so far even as to deny my existence. In order,
therefore, that I may know that I exist, I resort to Descartes's

method: "I think, therefore I am." Thus I am metaphysically established, and I throw upon the doubters the burden of proving my non-existence. When we consider how little has been found out about the mind, is it not amazing that any one should presume to define what one can know or cannot know? I admit that there are innumerable marvels in the visible universe unguessed by me. Likewise, O confident critic, there are a myriad sensations perceived by me of which you do not dream.

Necessity gives to the eye a precious power of seeing, and in the same way it gives a precious power of feeling to the whole body. Sometimes it seems as if the very substance of my flesh were so many eyes looking out at will upon a world new created every day. The silence and darkness which are said to shut me in, open my door most hospitably to countless sensations that distract, inform, admonish, and amuse. With my three trusty guides, touch, smell, and taste, I make many excursions into the borderland of experience which is in sight of the city of Light. Nature accommodates itself to every man's necessity. If the eye is maimed, so that it does not see the beauteous face of day, the touch becomes more poignant and discriminating. Nature proceeds through practice to strengthen and augment the remaining senses. For this reason the blind often hear with greater ease and distinctness than other people. The sense of smell becomes almost a new faculty to penetrate the tangle and vagueness of things. Thus, according to an immutable law, the senses assist and reinforce one another.

It is not for me to say whether we see best with the hand or the eye. I only know that the world I see with my fingers is alive, ruddy, and satisfying. Touch brings the blind many sweet certainties which our more fortunate fellows miss, because their sense of touch is uncultivated. When they look at things, they put their hands in their pockets. No doubt that is one reason why their knowledge is often so vague, inaccurate, and useless. It is probable, too, that our knowledge of phenomena beyond the reach of the hand is equally imperfect. But, at all events, we behold them through a golden mist of fantasy.

There is nothing, however, misty or uncertain about what we can touch. Through the sense of touch I know the faces of friends, the illimitable variety of straight and curved lines, all surfaces, the exuberance of the soil, the delicate shapes of flowers, the noble forms of trees, and the range of mighty winds. Besides objects, surfaces, and atmospherical changes, I perceive countless vibrations. I derive much knowledge of everyday matter from the jars and jolts which are to be felt everywhere in the house.

Footsteps, I discover, vary tactually according to the age, the sex, and the manners of the walker. It is impossible to mistake a child's patter for the tread of a grown person. The step of the young man, strong and free, differs from the heavy, sedate tread of the middle-aged, and from the step of the old man, whose feet drag along the floor, or beat it with slow, faltering accents. On a bare floor a girl walks with a rapid, elastic rhythm which is quite distinct from the graver step of the elderly woman. I have laughed over the creak of new shoes and the clatter of a stout maid performing a jig in the kitchen. One day, in the dining-room of a hotel, a tactual dissonance arrested my attention. I sat still and listened with my feet. I found that two waiters were walking back and forth, but not with the same gait. A band was playing, and I could feel the music-waves along the floor. One of the waiters walked in time to the band, graceful and light, while the other disregarded the music and rushed from table to table to the beat of some discord in his own mind. Their steps reminded me of a spirited war-steed harnessed with a cart-horse.

Often footsteps reveal in some measure the character and the mood of the walker. I feel in them firmness and indecision, hurry and deliberation, activity and laziness, fatigue, carelessness, timidity, anger, and sorrow. I am most conscious of these moods and traits in persons with whom I am familiar.

Footsteps are frequently interrupted by certain jars and jerks, so that I know when one kneels, kicks, shakes something, sits down, or gets up. Thus I follow to some extent the actions of people about me and the changes of their postures. Just now a thick, soft patter of bare, padded feet and a slight jolt told me that my dog had jumped on the chair to look out of the window. I do not, however, allow him to go uninvestigated; for occasionally I feel the same motion, and find him, not on the chair, but trespassing on the sofa.

When a carpenter works in the house or in the barn near by, I know by the slanting, up-and-down, toothed vibration, and the ringing concussion of blow upon blow, that he is sawing or hammering. If I am near enough, a certain vibration, traveling back and forth along a wooden surface, brings me the information that he is using a plane.

A slight flutter on the rug tells me that a breeze has blown my papers off the table. A round thump is a signal that a pencil has rolled on the floor. If a book falls, it gives a flat thud. A wooden rap on the balustrade announces that dinner is ready. Many of these vibrations are obliterated out of doors. On a lawn or the road, I can feel only running, stamping, and the rumble of wheels.

By placing my hand on a person's lips and throat, I gain an idea of many specific vibrations, and interpret them: a boy's chuckle, a man's "Whew!" of surprise, the "Hem!" of annoyance or perplexity, the moan of pain, a scream, a whisper, a rasp, a sob, a choke, and a gasp. The utterances of animals, though wordless, are eloquent to me—the cat's purr, its mew, its angry, jerky, scolding spit; the dog's bow-wow of warning or of joyous welcome, its yelp of despair, and its contented snore; the cow's moo; a monkey's chatter; the snort of a horse; the lion's roar, and the terrible snarl of the tiger. Perhaps I ought to add, for the benefit of the critics and doubters who may peruse this essay, that with my own hand I have felt all these sounds. From my childhood to the present day I have availed myself of every opportunity to visit zoölogical gardens, menageries, and the circus, and all the animals, except the tiger, have talked into my hand. I have touched the tiger only in a museum, where he is as harmless as a lamb. I have, however, heard him talk by putting my hand on the bars of his cage. I have touched several lions in the flesh, and felt them roar royally, like a cataract over rocks.

To continue, I know the *plop* of liquid in a pitcher. So if I spill my milk, I have not the excuse of ignorance. I am also familiar with the pop of a cork, the sputter of a flame, the tick-tack of the clock, the metallic swing of the windmill, the labored rise and fall of the pump, the voluminous spurt of the hose, the deceptive tap of the breeze at door and window, and many other vibrations past computing.

There are tactual vibrations which do not belong to skin-touch. They penetrate the skin, the nerves, the bones, like pain, heat, and cold. The beat of a drum smites me through from the chest to the shoulder-blades. The din of the train, the bridge, and grinding machinery retains its "old-man-of-the-sea" grip upon me long after its cause has been left behind. If vibration and motion combine in my touch for any length of time, the earth seems to run away while I stand still. When I step off the train, the platform whirls round, and I find it difficult to walk steadily.

Every atom of my body is a vibroscope. But my sensations are not infallible. I reach out, and my fingers meet something furry, which jumps about, gathers itself together as if to spring, and acts like an animal. I pause a moment for caution. I touch it again more firmly, and find it is a fur coat fluttering and flapping in the wind. To me, as to you, the earth seems motionless, and the sun appears to move; for the rays of the afternoon withdraw more and more, as they touch my face, until the air becomes cool. From this I understand how it is that the shore seems to recede as you sail away from it. Hence I feel no incredulity when you say that parallel lines appear to converge, and the earth and sky to meet. My few senses long ago revealed to me their imperfections and deceptivity.

Not only are the senses deceptive, but numerous usages in our language indicate that people who have five senses find it difficult to keep their functions distinct. I understand that we hear views, see tones, taste music. I am told that voices have color. Tact, which I had supposed to be a matter of nice perception, turns out to be a matter of taste. Judging from the large use of the word, taste appears to be the most important of all the senses. Taste governs the great and small conventions of life. Certainly the language of the senses is full of contradictions, and my fellows who have five doors to their house are not more surely at home in themselves than I. May I not, then, be excused if this account of my sensations lacks precision?

V. The Finer Vibrations

I HAVE spoken of the numerous jars and jolts which daily minister to my faculties. The loftier and grander vibrations which appeal to my emotions are varied and abundant. I listen with awe to the roll of the thunder and the muffled avalanche of sound when the sea flings itself upon the shore. And I love the instrument by which all the diapasons of the ocean are caught and released in surging floods—the many-voiced organ. If music could be seen, I could point where the organ-notes go, as they rise and fall, climb up and up, rock and sway, now loud and deep, now high and stormy, anon soft and solemn, with lighter vibrations interspersed between and running across them. I should say that organ-music fills to an ecstasy the act of feeling.

There is tangible delight in other instruments, too. The violin seems beautifully alive as it responds to the lightest wish of the master. The distinction between its notes is more delicate than between the notes of the piano.

I enjoy the music of the piano most when I touch the instrument. If I keep my hand on the piano-case, I detect tiny quavers, returns of melody, and the hush that follows. This explains to me how sound can die away to the listening ear:

> . . . How thin and clear,
> And thinner, clearer, farther going!
> O sweet and far from cliff and scar
> The horns of Elfland faintly blowing!

I am able to follow the dominant spirit and mood of the music. I catch the joyous dance as it bounds over the keys, the slow

21

dirge, the reverie. I thrill to the fiery sweep of notes crossed by thunderous tones in the "Walküre," where *Wotan* kindles the dread flames that guard the sleeping *Brunhild.* How wonderful is the instrument on which a great musician sings with his hands! I have never succeeded in distinguishing one composition from another. I think this is possible; but the concentration and strain upon my attention would be so great that I doubt if the pleasure derived would be commensurate to the effort.

Nor can I distinguish easily a tune that is sung. But by placing my hand on another's throat and cheek, I enjoy the changes of the voice. I know when it is low or high, clear or muffled, sad or cheery. The thin, quavering sensation of an old voice differs in my touch from the sensation of a young voice. A Southerner's drawl is quite unlike the Yankee twang. Sometimes the flow and ebb of a voice is so enchanting that my fingers quiver with exquisite pleasure, even if I do not understand a word that is spoken.

On the other hand, I am exceedingly sensitive to the harshness of noises like grinding, scraping, and the hoarse creak of rusty locks. Fog-whistles are my vibratory nightmares. I have stood near a bridge in process of construction, and felt the tactual din, the rattle of heavy masses of stone, the roll of loosened earth, the rumble of engines, the dumping of dirt-cars, the triple blows of vulcan hammers. I can also smell the fire-pots, the tar and cement. So I have a vivid idea of mighty labors in steel and stone, and I believe that I am acquainted with all the fiendish noises which can be made by man or machinery. The whack of heavy falling bodies, the sudden shivering splinter of chopped logs, the crystal shatter of pounded ice, the crash of a tree hurled to the earth by a hurricane, the irrational, persistent chaos of noise made by switching freight-trains, the explosion of gas, the blasting of stone, and the terrific grinding of rock upon rock which precedes the collapse—all these have been in my touch-experience, and contribute to my idea of Bedlam, of a battle, a waterspout, an earthquake, and other enormous accumulations of sound.

Touch brings me into contact with the traffic and manifold activity of the city. Besides the bustle and crowding of people

and the nondescript grating and electric howling of street-cars, I
am conscious of exhalations from many different kinds of shops;
from automobiles, drays, horses, fruit stands, and many varieties
of smoke.

> Odors strange and musty,
> The air sharp and dusty
> With lime and with sand,
> That no one can stand,
> Make the street impassable,
> The people irascible,
> Until every one cries,
> As he trembling goes
> With the sight of his eyes
> And the scent of his nose
> Quite stopped—or at least much diminished—
> "Gracious! when will this city be finished?"[1]

The city is interesting; but the tactual silence of the country
is always most welcome after the din of town and the irritating
concussions of the train. How noiseless and undisturbing are
the demolition, the repairs and the alterations, of nature! With
no sound of hammer or saw or stone severed from stone, but
a music of rustles and ripe thumps on the grass come the fluttering leaves and mellow fruits which the wind tumbles all day
from the branches. Silently all droops, all withers, all is poured
back into the earth that it may recreate; all sleeps while the busy
architects of day and night ply their silent work elsewhere. The
same serenity reigns when all at once the soil yields up a newly
wrought creation. Softly the ocean of grass, moss, and flowers
rolls surge upon surge across the earth. Curtains of foliage drape
the bare branches. Great trees make ready in their sturdy hearts
to receive again birds which occupy their spacious chambers to
the south and west. Nay, there is no place so lowly that it may
not lodge some happy creature. The meadow brook undoes its
icy fetters with rippling notes, gurgles, and runs free. And all

---

[1] George Arnold.

this is wrought in less than two months to the music of nature's orchestra, in the midst of balmy incense.

The thousand soft voices of the earth have truly found their way to me—the small rustle in tufts of grass, the silky swish of leaves, the buzz of insects, the hum of bees in blossoms I have plucked, the flutter of a bird's wings after his bath, and the slender rippling vibration of water running over pebbles. Once having been felt, these loved voices rustle, buzz, hum, flutter, and ripple in my thought forever, an undying part of happy memories.

Between my experiences and the experiences of others there is no gulf of mute space which I may not bridge. For I have endlessly varied, instructive contacts with all the world, with life, with the atmosphere whose radiant activity enfolds us all. The thrilling energy of the all-encasing air is warm and rapturous. Heat-waves and sound-waves play upon my face in infinite variety and combination, until I am able to surmise what must be the myriad sounds that my senseless ears have not heard.

The air varies in different regions, at different seasons of the year, and even different hours of the day. The odorous, fresh sea-breezes are distinct from the fitful breezes along river banks, which are humid and freighted with inland smells. The bracing, light, dry air of the mountains can never be mistaken for the pungent salt air of the ocean. The air of winter is dense, hard, compressed. In the spring it has new vitality. It is light, mobile, and laden with a thousand palpitating odors from earth, grass, and sprouting leaves. The air of midsummer is dense, saturated, or dry and burning, as if it came from a furnace. When a cool breeze brushes the sultry stillness, it brings fewer odors than in May, and frequently the odor of a coming tempest. The avalanche of coolness which sweeps through the low-hanging air bears little resemblance to the stinging coolness of winter.

The rain of winter is raw, without odor and dismal. The rain of spring is brisk, fragrant, charged with life-giving warmth. I welcome it delightedly as it visits the earth, enriches the streams, waters the hills abundantly, makes the furrows soft with showers for the seed, elicits a perfume which I cannot breathe deep enough. Spring rain is beautiful, impartial, lovable. With pearly drops it washes every leaf on tree and bush, ministers equally to salutary herbs and noxious growths, searches out every living thing that needs its beneficence.

The senses assist and reinforce each other to such an extent that I am not sure whether touch or smell tells me the most about the world. Everywhere the river of touch is joined by the brooks of odor-perception. Each season has its distinctive odors. The spring is earthy and full of sap. July is rich with the odor of ripening grain and hay. As the season advances, a crisp, dry, mature odor predominates, and golden-rod, tansy, and everlastings mark the onward march of the year. In autumn, soft, alluring scents fill the air, floating from thicket, grass, flower, and tree, and they tell me of time and change, of death and life's renewal, desire and its fulfilment.

VI. Smell, the Fallen Angel

FOR some inexplicable reason the sense of smell does not hold the high position it deserves among its sisters. There is something of the fallen angel about it. When it woos us with woodland scents and beguiles us with the fragrance of lovely gardens, it is admitted frankly to our discourse. But when it gives us warning of something noxious in our vicinity, it is treated as if the demon had got the upper hand of the angel, and is relegated to outer darkness, punished for its faithful service. It is most difficult to keep the true significance of words when one discusses the prejudices of mankind, and I find it hard to give an account of odor-perceptions which shall be at once dignified and truthful.

In my experience smell is most important, and I find that there is high authority for the nobility of the sense which we have neglected and disparaged. It is recorded that the Lord commanded that incense be burnt before him continually with a sweet savor. I doubt if there is any sensation arising from sight more delightful than the odors which filter through sun-warmed, wind-tossed branches, or the tide of scents which swells, subsides, rises again wave on wave, filling the wide world with invisible sweetness. A whiff of the universe makes us dream of worlds we have never seen, recalls in a flash entire epochs of our dearest experience. I never smell daisies without living over again the ecstatic mornings that my teacher and I spent wandering in the fields, while I learned new words and the names of things. Smell is a potent wizard that transports us across a thousand miles and all the years we have lived. The odor of fruits wafts me to my Southern home, to my childish frolics in the peach orchard. Other odors, instantaneous and fleeting, cause my heart to dilate joyously or contract with remembered grief. Even as I think of smells, my nose is full of scents that start awake sweet memories of summers gone and ripening grain fields far away.

The faintest whiff from a meadow where the new-mown hay lies in the hot sun displaces the here and the now. I am back again in the old red barn. My little friends and I are playing in the haymow. A huge mow it is, packed with crisp, sweet hay, from the top of which the smallest child can reach the straining rafters. In their stalls beneath are the farm animals. Here is Jerry, unresponsive, unbeautiful Jerry, crunching his oats like a true pessimist, resolved to find his feed not good—at least not so good as it ought to be. Again I touch Brownie, eager, grateful little Brownie, ready to leave the juiciest fodder for a pat, straining his beautiful, slender neck for a caress. Near by stands Lady Belle, with sweet, moist mouth, lazily extracting the sealed-up cordial from timothy and clover, and dreaming of deep June pastures and murmurous streams.

The sense of smell has told me of a coming storm hours before there was any sign of it visible. I notice first a throb of expectancy, a slight quiver, a concentration in my nostrils. As the storm draws nearer, my nostrils dilate the better to receive the flood of earth-odors which seem to multiply and extend, until I feel the splash of rain against my cheek. As the tempest departs, receding farther and farther, the odors fade, become fainter and fainter, and die away beyond the bar of space.

I know by smell the kind of house we enter. I have recognized an old-fashioned country house because it has several layers of odors, left by a succession of families, of plants, perfumes, and draperies.

In the evening quiet there are fewer vibrations than in the daytime, and then I rely more largely upon smell. The sulphuric scent of a match tells me that the lamps are being lighted.

Later I note the wavering trail of odor that flits about and disappears. It is the curfew signal; the lights are out for the night.

Out of doors I am aware by smell and touch of the ground we tread and the places we pass. Sometimes, when there is no wind, the odors are so grouped that I know the character of the country, and can place a hayfield, a country store, a garden, a barn, a grove of pines, a farmhouse with the windows open.

The other day I went to walk toward a familiar wood. Suddenly a disturbing odor made me pause in dismay. Then followed a peculiar, measured jar, followed by dull, heavy thunder. I understood the odor and the jar only too well. The trees were being cut down. We climbed the stone wall to the left. It borders the wood which I have loved so long that it seems to be my peculiar possession. But to-day an unfamiliar rush of air and an unwonted outburst of sun told me that my tree friends were gone. The place was empty, like a deserted dwelling. I stretched out my hand. Where once stood the steadfast pines, great, beautiful, sweet, my hand touched raw, moist stumps. All about lay broken branches, like the antlers of stricken deer. The fragrant, piled-up sawdust swirled and tumbled about me. An unreasoning resentment flashed through me at this ruthless destruction of the beauty that I love. But there is no anger, no resentment in nature. The air is equally charged with the odors of life and of destruction, for death equally with growth forever ministers to all-conquering life. The sun shines as ever, and the winds riot through the newly opened spaces. I know that a new forest will spring where the old one stood, as beautiful, as beneficent.

Touch sensations are permanent and definite. Odors deviate and are fugitive, changing in their shades, degrees, and location. There is something else in odor which gives me a sense of distance. I should call it horizon—the line where odor and fancy meet at the farthest limit of scent.

Smell gives me more idea than touch or taste of the manner in which sight and hearing probably discharge their functions.

"Listening" to the Trees

Touch seems to reside in the object touched, because there is a contact of surfaces. In smell there is no notion of relievo, and odor seems to reside not in the object smelt, but in the organ. Since I smell a tree at a distance, it is comprehensible to me that a person sees it without touching it. I am not puzzled over the fact that he receives it as an image on his retina without relievo, since my smell perceives the tree as a thin sphere with no fullness or content. By themselves, odors suggest nothing. I must learn by association to judge from them of distance, of place, and of the actions or the surroundings which are the usual occasions for them, just as I am told people judge from color, light, and sound.

From exhalations I learn much about people. I often know the work they are engaged in. The odors of wood, iron, paint, and drugs cling to the garments of those that work in them. Thus I can distinguish the carpenter from the ironworker, the artist from the mason or the chemist. When a person passes quickly from one place to another I get a scent impression of where he has been—the kitchen, the garden, or the sick-room. I gain pleasurable ideas of freshness and good taste from the odors of soap, toilet water, clean garments, woollen and silk stuffs, and gloves.

I have not, indeed, the all-knowing scent of the hound or the wild animal. None but the halt and the blind need fear my skill in pursuit; for there are other things besides water, stale trails, confusing cross tracks to put me at fault. Nevertheless, human odors are as varied and capable of recognition as hands and faces. The dear odors of those I love are so definite, so unmistakable, that nothing can quite obliterate them. If many years should elapse before I saw an intimate friend again, I think I should recognize his odor instantly in the heart of Africa, as promptly as would my brother that barks.

Once, long ago, in a crowded railway station, a lady kissed me as she hurried by. I had not touched even her dress. But she left a scent with her kiss which gave me a glimpse of her. The years are many since she kissed me. Yet her odor is fresh in my memory.

It is difficult to put into words the thing itself, the elusive person-odor. There seems to be no adequate vocabulary of smells, and I must fall back on approximate phrase and metaphor.

Some people have a vague, unsubstantial odor that floats about, mocking every effort to identify it. It is the will-o'-the-wisp of my olfactive experience. Sometimes I meet one who lacks a distinctive person-scent, and I seldom find such a one lively or entertaining. On the other hand, one who has a pungent odor often possesses great vitality, energy, and vigor of mind.

Masculine exhalations are as a rule stronger, more vivid, more widely differentiated than those of women. In the odor of young men there is something elemental, as of fire, storm, and salt sea. It pulsates with buoyancy and desire. It suggests all things strong and beautiful and joyous, and gives me a sense of physical happiness. I wonder if others observe that all infants have the same scent—pure, simple, undecipherable as their dormant personality. It is not until the age of six or seven that they begin to have perceptible individual odors. These develop and mature along with their mental and bodily powers.

What I have written about smell, especially person-smell, will perhaps be regarded as the abnormal sentiment of one who can have no idea of the "world of reality and beauty which the eye perceives." There are people who are color-blind, people who are tone-deaf. Most people are smell-blind-and-deaf. We should not condemn a musical composition on the testimony of an ear which cannot distinguish one chord from another, or judge a picture by the verdict of a color-blind critic. The sensations of smell which cheer, inform, and broaden my life are not less pleasant merely because some critic who treads the wide, bright pathway of the eye has not cultivated his olfactive sense. Without the shy, fugitive, often unobserved, sensations and the certainties which taste, smell, and touch give me, I should be obliged to take my conception of the universe wholly from others. I should lack the alchemy by which I now infuse into my world light, color, and the Protean spark. The sensuous reality which interthreads and supports all the gropings of my imagination would be shattered. The solid earth would melt from under my feet and disperse itself in space. The objects dear to my hands would become formless, dead things, and I should walk among them as among invisible ghosts.

VII. Relative Values of the Senses

I WAS once without the sense of smell and taste for several days. It seemed incredible, this utter detachment from odors, to breathe the air in and observe never a single scent. The feeling was probably similar, though less in degree, to that of one who first loses sight and cannot but expect to see the light again any day, any minute. I knew I should smell again some time. Still, after the wonder had passed off, a loneliness crept over me as vast as the air whose myriad odors I missed. The multitudinous subtle delights that smell makes mine became for a time wistful memories. When I recovered the lost sense, my heart bounded with gladness. It is a fine dramatic touch that Hans Andersen gives to the story of Kay and Gerda in the passage about flowers. Kay, whom the wicked magician's glass has blinded to human love, rushes away fiercely from home when he discovers that the roses have lost their sweetness.

The loss of smell for a few days gave me a clearer idea than I had ever had what it is to be blinded suddenly, helplessly. With a little stretch of the imagination I knew then what it must be when the great curtain shuts out suddenly the light of day, the stars, and the firmament itself. I see the blind man's eyes strain for the light, as he fearfully tries to walk his old rounds, until the unchanging blank that everywhere spreads before him stamps the reality of the dark upon his consciousness.

My temporary loss of smell proved to me, too, that the absence of a sense need not dull the mental faculties and does not distort one's view of the world, and so I reason that blindness and deafness need not pervert the inner order of the intellect. I know that if there were no odors for me I should still possess

33

a considerable part of the world. Novelties and surprises would abound, adventures would thicken in the dark.

In my classification of the senses, smell is a little the ear's inferior, and touch is a great deal the eye's superior. I find that great artists and philosophers agree with me in this. Diderot says:

> Je trouvais que de tous les sens, l'œil était le plus superficiel; l'oreille, le plus orgueilleux; l'odorat, le plus voluptueux; le goût, le plus superstitieux et le plus inconstant; le toucher, le plus profond et le plus philosophe.[1]

A friend whom I have never seen sends me a quotation from Symonds's "Renaissance in Italy":

> Lorenzo Ghiberti, after describing a piece of antique sculpture he saw in Rome adds, "To express the perfection of learning, mastery, and art displayed in it is beyond the power of language. Its more exquisite beauties could not be discovered by the sight, but only by the touch of the hand passed over it." Of another classic marble at Padua he says, "This statue, when the Christian faith triumphed, was hidden in that place by some gentle soul, who, seeing it so perfect, fashioned with art so wonderful, and with such power of genius, and being moved to reverent pity, caused a sepulchre of bricks to be built, and there within buried the statue, and covered it with a broad slab of stone, that it might not in any way be injured. It has very many sweet beauties which the eyes alone can comprehend not, either by strong or tempered light; only the hand by touching them finds them out."

Hold out your hands to feel the luxury of the sunbeams. Press the soft blossoms against your cheek, and finger their graces of form, their delicate mutability of shape, their pliancy and freshness. Expose your face to the aërial floods that sweep the heavens, "inhale great draughts of space," wonder, wonder at the wind's unwearied activity. Pile note on note the infinite music

---

[1] I found that of the senses, the eye is the most superficial, the ear the most arrogant, smell the most voluptuous, taste the most superstitious and fickle, touch the most profound and the most philosophical.

that flows increasingly to your soul from the tactual sonorities of a thousand branches and tumbling waters. How can the world be shriveled when this most profound, emotional sense, touch, is faithful to its service? I am sure that if a fairy bade me choose between the sense of sight and that of touch, I would not part with the warm, endearing contact of human hands or the wealth of form, the mobility and fullness that press into my palms.

VIII. The Five-Sensed World

THE poets have taught us how full of wonders is the night; and the night of blindness has its wonders, too. The only lightless dark is the night of ignorance and insensibility. We differ, blind and seeing, one from another, not in our senses, but in the use we make of them, in the imagination and courage with which we seek wisdom beyond our senses.

It is more difficult to teach ignorance to think than to teach an intelligent blind man to see the grandeur of Niagara. I have walked with people whose eyes are full of light, but who see nothing in wood, sea, or sky, nothing in city streets, nothing in books. What a witless masquerade is this seeing! It were better far to sail forever in the night of blindness, with sense and feeling and mind, than to be thus content with the mere act of seeing. They have the sunset, the morning skies, the purple of distant hills, yet their souls voyage through this enchanted world with a barren stare.

The calamity of the blind is immense, irreparable. But it does not take away our share of the things that count—service, friendship, humor, imagination, wisdom. It is the secret inner will that controls one's fate. We are capable of willing to be good, of loving and being loved, of thinking to the end that we may be wiser. We possess these spirit-born forces equally with all God's children. Therefore we, too, see the lightnings and hear the thunders of Sinai. We, too, march through the wilderness and the solitary place that shall be glad for us, and as we pass, God maketh the desert to blossom like the rose. We, too, go in unto the Promised Land to possess the treasures of the spirit, the unseen permanence of life and nature.

The blind man of spirit faces the unknown and grapples with it, and what else does the world of seeing men do? He has imagination, sympathy, humanity, and these ineradicable existences compel him to share by a sort of proxy in a sense he has not. When he meets terms of color, light, physiognomy, he guesses, divines, puzzles out their meaning by analogies drawn from the senses he has. I naturally tend to think, reason, draw inferences as if I had five senses instead of three. This tendency is beyond my control; it is involuntary, habitual, instinctive. I cannot compel my mind to say "I feel" instead of "I see" or "I hear." The word "feel" proves on examination to be no less a convention than "see" and "hear" when I seek for words accurately to describe the outward things that affect my three bodily senses. When a man loses a leg, his brain persists in impelling him to use what he has not and yet feels to be there. Can it be that the brain is so constituted that it will continue the activity which animates the sight and the hearing, after the eye and the ear have been destroyed?

It might seem that the five senses would work intelligently together only when resident in the same body. Yet when two or three are left unaided, they reach out for their complements in another body, and find that they yoke easily with the borrowed team. When my hand aches from overtouching, I find relief in the sight of another. When my mind lags, wearied with the strain of forcing out thoughts about dark, musicless, colorless, detached substance, it recovers its elasticity as soon as I resort to the powers of another mind which commands light, harmony, color. Now, if the five senses will not remain disassociated, the life of the deaf-blind cannot be severed from the life of the seeing, hearing race.

The deaf-blind person may be plunged and replunged like Schiller's diver into seas of the unknown. But, unlike the doomed hero, he returns triumphant, grasping the priceless truth that his mind is not crippled, not limited to the infirmity of his senses. The world of the eye and the ear becomes to him a subject of fateful interest. He seizes every word of sight and hearing because his sensations compel it. Light and color, of which he has no tactual evidence, he studies fearlessly, believing that all humanly knowable truth is open to him. He is in a position similar to that of the astronomer who, firm, patient, watches a star night after night for many years and feels rewarded if he discovers a single fact about it. The man deaf-blind to ordinary outward things, and the man deaf-blind to the immeasurable universe, are both limited by time and space; but they have made a compact to wring service from their limitations.

The bulk of the world's knowledge is an imaginary construction. History is but a mode of imagining, of making us see civilizations that no longer appear upon the earth. Some of the most significant discoveries in modern science owe their origin to the imagination of men who had neither accurate knowledge nor exact instruments to demonstrate their beliefs. If astronomy had not kept always in advance of the telescope, no one would ever have thought a telescope worth making. What great invention has not existed in the inventor's mind long before he gave it tangible shape?

A more splendid example of imaginative knowledge is the unity with which philosophers start their study of the world. They can never perceive the world in its entire reality. Yet their imagination, with its magnificent allowance for error, its power of treating uncertainty as negligible, has pointed the way for empirical knowledge.

In their highest creative moments the great poet, the great musician cease to use the crude instruments of sight and hearing. They break away from their sense-moorings, rise on strong, compelling wings of spirit far above our misty hills and darkened valleys into the region of light, music, intellect.

What eye hath seen the glories of the New Jerusalem? What ear hath heard the music of the spheres, the steps of time, the strokes of chance, the blows of death? Men have not heard with their physical sense the tumult of sweet voices above the hills of Judea nor seen the heavenly vision; but millions have listened to that spiritual message through many ages.

Our blindness changes not a whit the course of inner realities.

Of us it is as true as it is of the seeing that the most beautiful world is always entered through the imagination. If you wish to be something that you are not,—something fine, noble, good,—you shut your eyes, and for one dreamy moment you are that which you long to be.

IX. Inward Visions

ACCORDING to all art, all nature, all coherent human thought, we know that order, proportion, form, are essential elements of beauty. Now order, proportion, and form, are palpable to the touch. But beauty and rhythm are deeper than sense. They are like love and faith. They spring out of a spiritual process only slightly dependent upon sensations. Order, proportion, form, cannot generate in the mind the abstract idea of beauty, unless there is already a soul intelligence to breathe life into the elements. Many persons, having perfect eyes, are blind in their perceptions. Many persons, having perfect ears, are emotionally deaf. Yet these are the very ones who dare to set limits to the vision of those who, lacking a sense or two, have will, soul, passion, imagination. Faith is a mockery if it teaches us not that we may construct a world unspeakably more complete and beautiful than the material world. And I, too, may construct my better world, for I am a child of God, an inheritor of a fragment of the Mind that created all worlds.

There is a consonance of all things, a blending of all that we know about the material world and the spiritual. It consists for me of all the impressions, vibrations, heat, cold, taste, smell, and the sensations which these convey to the mind, infinitely combined, interwoven with associated ideas and acquired knowledge. No thoughtful person will believe that what I said about the meaning of footsteps is strictly true of mere jolts and jars. It is an array of the spiritual in certain natural elements, tactual beats, and an acquired knowledge of physical habits and moral traits of highly organized human beings. What would odors signify if they were not associated with the time of the year, the place I live in, and the people I know?

The result of such a blending is sometimes a discordant trying of strings far removed from a melody, very far from a symphony. (For the benefit of those who must be reassured, I will say that I have felt a musician tuning his violin, that I have read about a symphony, and so have a fair intellectual perception of my metaphor.) But with training and experience the faculties gather up the stray notes and combine them into a full, harmonious whole. If the person who accomplishes this task is peculiarly gifted, we call him a poet. The blind and the deaf are not great poets, it is true. Yet now and again you find one deaf and blind who has attained to his royal kingdom of beauty.

I have a little volume of poems by a deaf-blind lady, Madame Bertha Galeron. Her poetry has versatility of thought. Now it is tender and sweet, now full of tragic passion and the sternness of destiny. Victor Hugo called her "La Grande Voyante." She has written several plays, two of which have been acted in Paris. The French Academy has crowned her work.

The infinite wonders of the universe are revealed to us in exact measure as we are capable of receiving them. The keenness of our vision depends not on how much we can see, but on how much we feel. Nor yet does mere knowledge create beauty. Nature sings her most exquisite songs to those who love her. She does not unfold her secrets to those who come only to gratify their desire of analysis, to gather facts, but to those who see in her manifold phenomena suggestions of lofty, delicate sentiments.

Am I to be denied the use of such adjectives as "freshness" and "sparkle," "dark" and "gloomy"? I have walked in the fields at early morning. I have felt a rose-bush laden with dew and fragrance. I have felt the curves and graces of my kitten at play. I have known the sweet, shy ways of little children. I have known the sad opposites of all these, a ghastly touch picture. Remember, I have sometimes traveled over a dusty road as far as my feet could go. At a sudden turn I have stepped upon starved, ignoble weeds, and reaching out my hands, I have touched a fair tree out of which a parasite had taken the life like a vampire. I have touched a pretty bird whose soft wings hung limp, whose little heart beat no more. I have wept over the feebleness and deformity of a child, lame, or born blind, or, worse still, mindless. If I had the genius of Thomson, I, too, could depict a "City of Dreadful Night" from mere touch sensations. From contrasts so irreconcilable can we fail to form an idea of beauty and know surely when we meet with loveliness?

Here is a sonnet eloquent of a blind man's power of vision:

THE MOUNTAIN TO THE PINE

Thou tall, majestic monarch of the wood,
   That standest where no wild vines dare to creep,
   Men call thee old, and say that thou hast stood
   A century upon my rugged steep;
Yet unto me thy life is but a day,
   When I recall the things that I have seen,—
   The forest monarchs that have passed away
   Upon the spot where first I saw thy green;
For I am older than the age of man,
   Or all the living things that crawl or creep,
   Or birds of air, or creatures of the deep;
I was the first dim outline of God's plan:
   Only the waters of the restless sea
   And the infinite stars in heaven are old to me.

I am glad my friend Mr. Stedman knew that poem while he was making his Anthology, for knowing it, so fine a poet and critic could not fail to give it a place in his treasure-house of American poetry. The poet, Mr. Clarence Hawkes, has been blind since childhood; yet he finds in nature hints of combinations for his mental pictures. Out of the knowledge and impressions that come to him he constructs a masterpiece which hangs upon the walls of his thought. And into the poet's house come all the true spirits of the world.

It was a rare poet who thought of the mountain as "the first dim outline of God's plan." That is the real wonder of the poem, and not that a blind man should speak so confidently of sky and sea. Our ideas of the sky are an accumulation of touch-glimpses, literary allusions, and the observations of others, with an emotional blending of all. My face feels only a tiny portion of the atmosphere; but I go through continuous space and feel the air at every point, every instant. I have been told about the distances from our earth to the sun, to the other planets, and to the fixed stars. I multiply a thousand times the utmost height and width that my touch compasses, and thus I gain a deep sense of the sky's immensity.

Move me along constantly over water, water, nothing but water, and you give me the solitude, the vastness of ocean which fills the eye. I have been in a little sail-boat on the sea, when the rising tide swept it toward the shore. May I not understand the poet's figure: "The green of spring overflows the earth like a tide?" I have felt the flame of a candle blow and flutter in the breeze. May I not, then, say: "Myriads of fireflies flit hither and thither in the dew-wet grass like little fluttering tapers"?

Combine the endless space of air, the sun's warmth, the prevalence of fitful odors, the clouds that are described to my understanding spirit, the frequent breaking through the soil of a brook or the expanse of the wind-ruffled lake, the tactual undulation of the hills, which I recall when I am far away from them, the towering trees upon trees as I walk by them, the bearings that I try to keep while others tell me the directions of the various points of the scenery, and you will begin to feel surer of my mental landscape. The utmost bound to which my thought will go with clearness is the horizon of my mind. From this horizon I imagine the one which the eye marks.

Touch cannot bridge distance,—it is fit only for the contact of surfaces,—but thought leaps the chasm. For this reason I am able to use words descriptive of objects distant from my senses. I have felt the rondure of the infant's tender form. I can apply this perception to the landscape and to the far-off hills.

X. Analogies in Sense Perception

I HAVE not touched the outline of a star nor the glory of the moon, but I believe that God has set two lights in my mind, the greater to rule by day and the lesser by night, and by them I know that I am able to navigate my life-bark, as certain of reaching the haven as he who steers by the North Star. Perhaps my sun shines not as yours. The colors that glorify my world, the blue of the sky, the green of the fields, may not correspond exactly with those you delight in; but they are none the less color to me. The sun does not shine for my physical eyes, nor does the lightning flash, nor do the trees turn green in the spring; but they have not therefore ceased to exist, any more than the landscape is annihilated when you turn your back on it.

I understand how scarlet can differ from crimson because I know that the smell of an orange is not the smell of a grape-fruit. I can also conceive that colors have shades, and guess what shades are. In smell and taste there are varieties not broad enough to be fundamental; so I call them shades. There are half a dozen roses near me. They all have the unmistakable rose scent; yet my nose tells me that they are not the same. The American Beauty is distinct from the Jacqueminot and La France. Odors in certain grasses fade as really to my sense as certain colors do to yours in the sun. The freshness of a flower in my hand is analogous to the freshness I taste in an apple newly picked. I make use of analogies like these to enlarge my conceptions of colors. Some analogies which I draw between qualities in surface and vibration, taste and smell, are drawn by others between sight, hearing, and touch. This fact encourages me to persevere, to try and bridge the gap between the eye and the hand.

Certainly I get far enough to sympathize with the delight that my kind feel in beauty they see and harmony they hear. This bond between humanity and me is worth keeping, even if the idea on which I base it prove erroneous.

Sweet, beautiful vibrations exist for my touch, even though they travel through other substances than air to reach me. So I imagine sweet, delightful sounds, and the artistic arrangement of them which is called music, and I remember that they travel through the air to the ear, conveying impressions somewhat like mine. I also know what tones are, since they are perceptible tactually in a voice. Now, heat varies greatly in the sun, in the fire, in hands, and in the fur of animals; indeed, there is such a thing for me as a cold sun. So I think of the varieties of light that touch the eye, cold and warm, vivid and dim, soft and glaring, but always light, and I imagine their passage through the air to an extensive sense, instead of to a narrow one like touch. From the experience I have had with voices I guess how the eye distinguishes shades in the midst of light. While I read the lips of a woman whose voice is soprano, I note a low tone or a glad tone in the midst of a high, flowing voice. When I feel my cheeks hot, I know that I am red. I have talked so much and read so much about colors that through no will of my own I attach meanings to them, just as all people attach certain meanings to abstract terms like hope, idealism, monotheism, intellect, which cannot be represented truly by visible objects, but which are understood from analogies between immaterial concepts and the ideas they awaken of external things. The force of association drives me to say that white is exalted and pure, green is exuberant, red suggests love or shame or strength. Without the color or its equivalent, life to me would be dark, barren, a vast blackness.

Thus through an inner law of completeness my thoughts are not permitted to remain colorless. It strains my mind to separate color and sound from objects. Since my education began I have always had things described to me with their colors and sounds by one with keen senses and a fine feeling for the significant. Therefore I habitually think of things as colored and resonant. Habit accounts for part. The soul sense accounts for another part. The brain with its five-sensed construction asserts its right and accounts for the rest. Inclusive of all, the unity of the world demands that color be kept in it, whether I have cognizance of it or not. Rather than be shut out, I take part in it by discussing it, imagining it, happy in the happiness of those near me who gaze at the lovely hues of the sunset or the rainbow.

My hand has its share in this multiple knowledge, but it must never be forgotten that with the fingers I see only a very small portion of a surface, and that I must pass my hand continually over it before my touch grasps the whole. It is still more important, however, to remember that my imagination is not tethered to certain points, locations, and distances. It puts all the parts together simultaneously as if it saw or knew instead of feeling them. Though I feel only a small part of my horse at a time,—my horse is nervous and does not submit to manual explorations,—yet, because I have many times felt hock, nose, hoof and mane, I can see the steeds of Phœbus Apollo coursing the heavens.

With such a power active it is impossible that my thought should be vague, indistinct. It must needs be potent, definite. This is really a corollary of the philosophical truth that the real world exists only for the mind. That is to say, I can never touch the world in its entirety; indeed, I touch less of it than the portion that others see or hear. But all creatures, all objects, pass into my brain entire, and occupy the same extent there that they do in material space. I declare that for me branched thoughts, instead of pines, wave, sway, rustle, make musical the ridges of mountains rising summit upon summit. Mention a rose too far away for me to smell it. Straightway a scent steals into my nostril, a form presses against my palm in all its dilating softness, with rounded petals, slightly curled edges, curving stem, leaves drooping. When I would fain view the world as a whole, it rushes into vision—man, beast, bird, reptile, fly, sky, ocean, mountains, plain, rock, pebble. The warmth of life, the reality of creation is over all—the throb of human hands, glossiness of fur, lithe windings of long bodies, poignant buzzing of insects, the ruggedness of the steeps as I climb them, the liquid mobility and boom of waves upon the rocks. Strange to say, try as I may, I cannot force my touch to pervade this universe in all directions. The moment I try, the whole vanishes; only small objects or narrow portions of a surface, mere touch-signs, a chaos of things scattered at random, remain. No thrill, no delight is excited thereby. Restore to the artistic, comprehensive internal sense its rightful domain, and you give me joy which best proves the reality.

XI. Before the Soul Dawn

BEFORE my teacher came to me, I did not know that I am. I lived in a world that was a no-world. I cannot hope to describe adequately that unconscious, yet conscious time of nothingness. I did not know that I knew aught, or that I lived or acted or desired. I had neither will nor intellect. I was carried along to objects and acts by a certain blind natural impetus. I had a mind which caused me to feel anger, satisfaction, desire. These two facts led those about me to suppose that I willed and thought. I can remember all this, not because I knew that it was so, but because I have tactual memory. It enables me to remember that I never contracted my forehead in the act of thinking. I never viewed anything beforehand or chose it. I also recall tactually the fact that never in a start of the body or a heart-beat did I feel that I loved or cared for anything. My inner life, then, was a blank without past, present, or future, without hope or anticipation, without wonder or joy or faith.

> It was not night—it was not day,
> . . .
> But vacancy absorbing space,
> And fixedness, without a place;
> There were no stars—no earth—no time—
> No check—no change—no good—no crime.

My dormant being had no idea of God or immortality, no fear of death.

I remember, also through touch, that I had a power of association. I felt tactual jars like the stamp of a foot, the opening of a window or its closing, the slam of a door. After repeatedly smelling rain and feeling the discomfort of wetness, I acted like those about me: I ran to shut the window. But that was not thought in any sense. It was the same kind of association that makes animals take shelter from the rain. From the same instinct of aping others, I folded the clothes that came from the laundry, and put mine away, fed the turkeys, sewed bead-eyes on my doll's face, and did many other things of which I have the tactual remembrance. When I wanted anything I liked,—ice-cream, for instance, of which I was very fond,—I had a delicious taste on my tongue (which, by the way, I never have now), and in my hand I felt the turning of the freezer. I made the sign, and my mother knew I wanted ice-cream. I "thought" and desired in my fingers. If I had made a man, I should certainly have put the brain and soul in his finger-tips. From reminiscences like these I conclude that it is the opening of the two faculties, freedom of will, or choice, and rationality, or the power of thinking from one thing to another, which makes it possible to come into being first as a child, afterwards as a man.

Since I had no power of thought, I did not compare one mental state with another. So I was not conscious of any change or process going on in my brain when my teacher began to instruct me. I merely felt keen delight in obtaining more easily what I wanted by means of the finger motions she taught me. I thought only of objects, and only objects I wanted. It was the turning of the freezer on a larger scale. When I learned the meaning of "I" and "me" and found that I was something, I began to think. Then consciousness first existed for me. Thus it was not the sense of touch that brought me knowledge. It was the awakening of my soul that first rendered my senses their value, their cognizance of objects, names, qualities, and properties. Thought made me conscious of love, joy, and all the emotions. I was eager to know, then to understand, afterward to reflect on what I knew and understood, and the blind impetus, which had before driven me hither and thither at the dictates of my sensations, vanished forever.

I cannot represent more clearly than any one else the gradual and subtle changes from first impressions to abstract ideas. But

I know that my physical ideas, that is, ideas derived from material objects, appear to me first in ideas similar to those of touch. Instantly they pass into intellectual meanings. Afterward the meaning finds expression in what is called "inner speech." When I was a child, my inner speech was inner spelling. Although I am even now frequently caught spelling to myself on my fingers, yet I talk to myself, too, with my lips, and it is true that when I first learned to speak, my mind discarded the finger-symbols and began to articulate. However, when I try to recall what some one has said to me, I am conscious of a hand spelling into mine.

It has often been asked what were my earliest impressions of the world in which I found myself. But one who thinks at all of his first impressions knows what a riddle this is. Our impressions grow and change unnoticed, so that what we suppose we thought as children may be quite different from what we actually experienced in our childhood. I only know that after my education began the world which came within my reach was all alive. I spelled to my blocks and my dogs. I sympathized with plants when the flowers were picked, because I thought it hurt them, and that they grieved for their lost blossoms. It was two years before I could be made to believe that my dogs did not understand what I said, and I always apologized to them when I ran into or stepped on them.

As my experiences broadened and deepened, the indeterminate, poetic feelings of childhood began to fix themselves in definite thoughts. Nature—the world I could touch—was folded and filled with myself. I am inclined to believe those philosophers who declare that we know nothing but our own feelings and ideas. With a little ingenious reasoning one may see in the material world simply a mirror, an image of permanent mental sensations. In either sphere self-knowledge is the condition and the limit of our consciousness. That is why, perhaps, many people know so little about what is beyond their short range of experience. They look within themselves—and find nothing! Therefore they conclude that there is nothing outside themselves, either.

However that may be, I came later to look for an image of my emotions and sensations in others. I had to learn the outward signs of inward feelings. The start of fear, the suppressed, controlled tensity of pain, the beat of happy muscles in others, had to be perceived and compared with my own experiences before I could trace them back to the intangible soul of another. Groping, uncertain, I at last found my identity, and after seeing my thoughts and feelings repeated in others, I gradually constructed my world of men and of God. As I read and study, I find that this is what the rest of the race has done. Man looks within himself and in time finds the measure and the meaning of the universe.

XII. The Larger Sanctions

So, in the midst of life, eager, imperious life, the deaf-blind child, fettered to the bare rock of circumstance, spider-like, sends out gossamer threads of thought into the measureless void that surrounds him. Patiently he explores the dark, until he builds up a knowledge of the world he lives in, and his soul meets the beauty of the world, where the sun shines always, and the birds sing. To the blind child the dark is kindly. In it he finds nothing extraordinary or terrible. It is his familiar world; even the groping from place to place, the halting steps, the dependence upon others, do not seem strange to him. He does not know how many countless pleasures the dark shuts out from him. Not until he weighs his life in the scale of others' experience does he realize what it is to live forever in the dark. But the knowledge that teaches him this bitterness also brings its consolation—spiritual light, the promise of the day that shall be.

The blind child—the deaf-blind child—has inherited the mind of seeing and hearing ancestors—a mind measured to five senses. Therefore he must be influenced, even if it be unknown to himself, by the light, color, song which have been transmitted through the language he is taught, for the chambers of the mind are ready to receive that language. The brain of the race is so permeated with color that it dyes even the speech of the blind. Every object I think of is stained with the hue that belongs to it by association and memory. The experience of the deaf-blind person, in a world of seeing, hearing people, is like that of a sailor on an island where the inhabitants speak a language unknown to him, whose life is unlike that he has lived. He is one, they are many; there is no chance of compromise. He must learn to see with their eyes, to hear with their ears, to think their thoughts, to follow their ideals.

If the dark, silent world which surrounds him were essentially different from the sunlit, resonant world, it would be incomprehensible to his kind, and could never be discussed. If his feelings and sensations were fundamentally different from those of others, they would be inconceivable except to those who had similar sensations and feelings. If the mental consciousness of the deaf-blind person were absolutely dissimilar to that of his fellows, he would have no means of imagining what they think. Since the mind of the sightless is essentially the same as that of the seeing in that it admits of no lack, it must supply some sort of equivalent for missing physical sensations. It must perceive a likeness between things outward and things inward, a correspondence between the seen and the unseen. I make use of such a correspondence in many relations, and no matter how far I pursue it to things I cannot see, it does not break under the test.

As a working hypothesis, correspondence is adequate to all life, through the whole range of phenomena. The flash of thought and its swiftness explain the lightning flash and the sweep of a comet through the heavens. My mental sky opens to me the vast celestial spaces, and I proceed to fill them with the images of my spiritual stars. I recognize truth by the clearness and guidance that it gives my thought, and, knowing what that clearness is, I can imagine what light is to the eye. It is not a convention of language, but a forcible feeling of the reality, that at times makes me start when I say, "Oh, I see my mistake!" or "How dark, cheerless is his life!" I know these are metaphors. Still, I must prove with them, since there is nothing in our language to replace them. Deaf-blind metaphors to correspond do not exist and are not necessary. Because I can understand the word "reflect" figuratively, a mirror has never perplexed me. The manner in which my imagination perceives absent things enables me to see how glasses can magnify things, bring them nearer, or remove them farther.

Deny me this correspondence, this internal sense, confine me to the fragmentary, incoherent touch-world, and lo, I become as

The Medallion

The bas-relief on the wall is a portrait of the Queen Dowager of Spain, which Her Majesty had made for Miss Keller.

a bat which wanders about on the wing. Suppose I omitted all words of seeing, hearing, color, light, landscape, the thousand phenomena, instruments and beauties connected with them. I should suffer a great diminution of the wonder and delight in attaining knowledge; also—more dreadful loss—my emotions would be blunted, so that I could not be touched by things unseen.

Has anything arisen to disprove the adequacy of correspondence? Has any chamber of the blind man's brain been opened and found empty? Has any psychologist explored the mind of the sightless and been able to say, "There is no sensation here?"

I tread the solid earth; I breathe the scented air. Out of these two experiences I form numberless associations and correspondences. I observe, I feel, I think, I imagine. I associate the countless varied impressions, experiences, concepts. Out of these materials Fancy, the cunning artisan of the brain, welds an image which the skeptic would deny me, because I cannot see with my physical eyes the changeful, lovely face of my thought-child. He would break the mind's mirror. This spirit-vandal would humble my soul and force me to bite the dust of material things. While I champ the bit of circumstance, he scourges and goads me with the spur of fact. If I heeded him, the sweet-visaged earth would vanish into nothing, and I should hold in my hand nought but an aimless, soulless lump of dead matter. But although the body physical is rooted alive to the Promethean rock, the spirit-proud huntress of the air will still pursue the shining, open highways of the universe.

Blindness has no limiting effect upon mental vision. My intellectual horizon is infinitely wide. The universe it encircles is immeasurable. Would they who bid me keep within the narrow bound of my meager senses demand of Herschel that he roof his stellar universe and give us back Plato's solid firmament of glassy spheres? Would they command Darwin from the grave and bid him blot out his geological time, give us back a paltry few thousand years? Oh, the supercilious doubters! They ever strive to clip the upward daring wings of the spirit.

A person deprived of one or more senses is not, as many

seem to think, turned out into a trackless wilderness without landmark or guide. The blind man carries with him into his dark environment all the faculties essential to the apprehension of the visible world whose door is closed behind him. He finds his surroundings everywhere homogeneous with those of the sunlit world; for there is an inexhaustible ocean of likenesses between the world within, and the world without, and these likenesses, these correspondences, he finds equal to every exigency his life offers.

The necessity of some such thing as correspondence or symbolism appears more and more urgent as we consider the duties that religion and philosophy enjoin upon us.

The blind are expected to read the Bible as a means of attaining spiritual happiness. Now, the Bible is filled throughout with references to clouds, stars, colors, and beauty, and often the mention of these is essential to the meaning of the parable or the message in which they occur. Here one must needs see the inconsistency of people who believe in the Bible, and yet deny us a right to talk about what we do not see, and for that matter what *they* do not see, either. Who shall forbid my heart to sing: "Yea, he did fly upon the wings of the wind. He made darkness his secret place; His pavilion round about him were dark waters and thick clouds of the skies"?

Philosophy constantly points out the untrustworthiness of the five senses and the important work of reason which corrects the errors of sight and reveals its illusions. If we cannot depend on five senses, how much less may we rely on three! What ground have we for discarding light, sound, and color as an integral part of our world? How are we to know that they have ceased to exist for us? We must take their reality for granted, even as the philosopher assumes the reality of the world without being able to see it physically as a whole.

Ancient philosophy offers an argument which seems still valid. There is in the blind as in the seeing an Absolute which gives truth to what we know to be true, order to what is orderly, beauty to the beautiful, touchableness to what is tangible. If this is granted, it follows that this Absolute is not imperfect, incomplete, partial. It must needs go beyond the limited evidence of our sensations, and also give light to what is invisible, music to the musical that silence dulls. Thus mind itself compels us to acknowledge that we are in a world of intellectual order, beauty, and harmony. The essences, or absolutes of these ideas, necessarily dispel their opposites which belong with evil, disorder and discord. Thus deafness and blindness do not exist in the immaterial mind, which is philosophically the real world, but are banished with the perishable material senses. Reality, of which visible things are the symbol, shines before my mind. While I walk about my chamber with unsteady steps, my spirit sweeps skyward on eagle wings and looks out with unquenchable vision upon the world of eternal beauty.

XIII. The Dream World

EVERYBODY takes his own dreams seriously, but yawns at the breakfast-table when somebody else begins to tell the adventures of the night before. I hesitate, therefore, to enter upon an account of my dreams; for it is a literary sin to bore the reader, and a scientific sin to report the facts of a far country with more regard to point and brevity than to complete and literal truth. The psychologists have trained a pack of theories and facts which they keep in leash, like so many bulldogs, and which they let loose upon us whenever we depart from the straight and narrow path of dream probability. One may not even tell an entertaining dream without being suspected of having liberally edited it,—as if editing were one of the seven deadly sins, instead of a useful and honorable occupation! Be it understood, then, that I am discoursing at my own breakfast-table, and that no scientific man is present to trip the autocrat.

I used to wonder why scientific men and others were always asking me about my dreams. But I am not surprised now, since I have discovered what some of them believe to be the ordinary waking experience of one who is both deaf and blind. They think that I can know very little about objects even a few feet beyond the reach of my arms. Everything outside of myself, according to them, is a hazy blur. Trees, mountains, cities, the ocean, even the house I live in are but fairy fabrications, misty unrealities. Therefore it is assumed that my dreams should have peculiar interest for the man of science. In some undefined way it is expected that they should reveal the world I dwell in to be flat, formless, colorless, without perspective, with little thickness and less solidity—a vast solitude of soundless space. But who shall put into words limitless, visionless, silent void? One should be a disembodied spirit indeed to make anything out of such insubstantial experiences. A world, or a dream for that matter, to be comprehensible to us, must, I should think, have a warp of substance woven into the woof of fantasy. We cannot imagine even in dreams an object which has no counterpart in reality. Ghosts always resemble somebody, and if they do not appear themselves, their presence is indicated by circumstances with which we are perfectly familiar.

During sleep we enter a strange, mysterious realm which science has thus far not explored. Beyond the border-line of slumber the investigator may not pass with his common-sense rule and test. Sleep with softest touch locks all the gates of our physical senses and lulls to rest the conscious will—the disciplinarian of our waking thoughts. Then the spirit wrenches itself free from the sinewy arms of reason and like a winged courser spurns the firm green earth and speeds away upon wind and cloud, leaving neither trace nor footprint by which science may track its flight and bring us knowledge of the distant, shadowy country that we nightly visit. When we come back from the dream-realm, we can give no reasonable report of what we met there. But once across the border, we feel at home as if we had always lived there and had never made any excursions into this rational daylight world.

My dreams do not seem to differ very much from the dreams of other people. Some of them are coherent and safely hitched to an event or a conclusion. Others are inconsequent and fantastic. All attest that in Dreamland there is no such thing as repose. We are always up and doing with a mind for any adventure. We act, strive, think, suffer and are glad to no purpose. We leave outside the portals of Sleep all troublesome incredulities and vexatious speculations as to probability. I float wraith-like upon clouds in and out among the winds, without the faintest notion that I am doing anything unusual. In Dreamland I find little that is altogether strange or wholly new to my experience. No matter what happens, I am not astonished, however extraordinary the circumstances may be. I visit a foreign land where I have not been in reality, and I converse with peoples whose language I have never heard. Yet we 'manage to understand each other perfectly. Into whatsoever situation or society my wanderings bring me, there is the same homogeneity. If I happen into Vagabondia, I make merry with the jolly folk of the road or the tavern.

I do not remember ever to have met persons with whom I could not at once communicate, or to have been shocked or surprised at the doings of my dream-companions. In its strange wanderings in those dusky groves of Slumberland my soul takes everything for granted and adapts itself to the wildest phantoms. I am seldom confused. Everything is as clear as day. I know events the instant they take place, and wherever I turn my steps, Mind is my faithful guide and interpreter.

I suppose every one has had in a dream the exasperating, profitless experience of seeking something urgently desired at the moment, and the aching, weary sensation that follows each failure to track the thing to its hiding-place. Sometimes with a singing dizziness in my head I climb and climb, I know not where or why. Yet I cannot quit the torturing, passionate endeavor, though again and again I reach out blindly for an object to hold to. Of course according to the perversity of dreams there is no object near. I clutch empty air, and then I fall downward, and still downward, and in the midst of the fall I dissolve into the atmosphere upon which I have been floating so precariously.

Some of my dreams seem to be traced one within another like a series of concentric circles. In sleep I think I cannot sleep. I toss about in the toils of tasks unfinished. I decide to get up and read for a while. I know the shelf in my library where I keep the book I want. The book has no name, but I find it without difficulty. I settle myself comfortably in the morris-chair, the great book open on my knee. Not a word can I make out, the pages are utterly blank. I am not surprised, but keenly disappointed. I finger the pages, I bend over them lovingly, the tears fall on my hands. I shut the book quickly as the thought passes through my mind, "The print will be all rubbed out if I get it wet." Yet there is no print tangible on the page!

This morning I thought that I awoke. I was certain that I had overslept. I seized my watch, and sure enough, it pointed to an hour after my rising time. I sprang up in the greatest hurry, knowing that breakfast was ready. I called my mother, who declared that my watch must be wrong. She was positive it could not be so late. I looked at my watch again, and lo! the hands wiggled, whirled, buzzed and disappeared. I awoke more fully as my dismay grew, until I was at the antipodes of sleep. Finally my eyes opened actually, and I knew that I had been dreaming. I had only waked into sleep. What is still more bewildering, there is no difference between the consciousness of the sham waking and that of the real one.

It is fearful to think that all that we have ever seen, felt, read, and done may suddenly rise to our dream-vision, as the sea casts up objects it has swallowed. I have held a little child in my arms in the midst of a riot and spoken vehemently, imploring the Russian soldiers not to massacre the Jews. I have re-lived the agonizing scenes of the Sepoy Rebellion and the French Revolution. Cities have burned before my eyes, and I have fought the flames until I fell exhausted. Holocausts overtake the world, and I struggle in vain to save my friends.

Once in a dream a message came speeding over land and sea that winter was descending upon the world from the North Pole, that the Arctic zone was shifting to our mild climate. Far and wide the message flew. The ocean was congealed in mid-summer. Ships were held fast in the ice by thousands, the ships with large, white sails were held fast. Riches of the Orient and the plenteous harvests of the Golden West might no more pass between nation and nation. For some time the trees and flowers grew on, despite the intense cold. Birds flew into the houses for safety, and those which winter had overtaken lay on the snow with wings spread in vain flight. At last the foliage and blossoms fell at the feet of Winter. The petals of the flowers were turned to rubies and sapphires. The leaves froze into emeralds. The trees moaned and tossed their branches as the frost pierced them through bark and sap, pierced into their very roots. I shivered myself awake, and with a tumult of joy I breathed the many sweet morning odors wakened by the summer sun.

One need not visit an African jungle or an Indian forest to hunt the tiger. One can lie in bed amid downy pillows and dream tigers as terrible as any in the pathless wild. I was a little girl when one night I tried to cross the garden in front of my aunt's house in Alabama. I was in pursuit of a large cat with a great bushy tail. A few hours before he had clawed my little canary out of its cage and crunched it between his cruel teeth. I could not see the cat. But the thought in my mind was distinct: "He is making for the high grass at the end of the garden. I'll get there first!" I put my hand on the box border and ran swiftly along the path. When I reached the high grass, there was the cat gliding into the wavy tangle. I rushed forward and tried to seize him and take the bird from between his teeth. To my horror a huge beast, not the cat at all, sprang out from the grass, and his sinewy shoulder rubbed against me with palpitating strength! His ears stood up and quivered with anger. His eyes were hot. His nostrils were large and wet. His lips moved horribly. I knew it was a tiger, a real live tiger, and that I should be devoured— my little bird and I. I do not know what happened after that. The next important thing seldom happens in dreams.

Some time earlier I had a dream which made a vivid impression upon me. My aunt was weeping because she could not find me. But I took an impish pleasure in the thought that she and others were searching for me, and making great noise which I felt through my feet. Suddenly the spirit of mischief gave way to uncertainty and fear. I felt cold. The air smelt like ice and salt. I tried to run; but the long grass tripped me, and I fell forward on my face. I lay very still, feeling with all my body. After a while my sensations seemed to be concentrated in my fingers, and I perceived that the grass blades were sharp as knives, and hurt my hands cruelly. I tried to get up cautiously, so as not to cut myself on the sharp grass. I put down a tentative foot, much as my kitten treads for the first time the primeval forest in the back yard. All at once I felt the stealthy patter of something creeping, creeping, creeping purposefully toward me. I do not know how at that time the idea was in my mind; I had no words for intention or purpose. Yet it was precisely the evil intent, and not the creeping animal that terrified me. I had no fear of living creatures. I loved my father's dogs, the frisky little calf, the gentle cows, the horses and mules that ate apples from my hand, and none of them had ever harmed me. I lay low, waiting in breathless terror for the creature to spring and bury its long claws in my flesh. I thought, "They will feel like turkey-claws." Something warm and wet touched my face. I shrieked, struck out frantically, and awoke. Something was still struggling in my arms. I held on with might and main until I was exhausted, then I loosed my hold. I found dear old Belle, the setter, shaking herself and looking at me reproachfully. She and I had gone to sleep together on the rug, and had naturally wandered to the dream-forest where dogs and little girls hunt wild game and have strange adventures. We encountered hosts of elfin foes, and it required all the dog tactics at Belle's command to acquit herself like the lady and huntress that she was. Belle had her dreams too. We used to lie under the trees and flowers in the old garden, and I used to laugh with delight when the magnolia leaves fell with little thuds, and Belle jumped up, thinking she had heard a partridge. She would pursue the leaf, point it, bring it back to me and lay it at my feet with a humorous wag of her tail as much as to say, "This is the kind of bird that waked me." I made a chain for her neck out of the lovely blue Paulownia flowers and covered her with great heart-shaped leaves.

Dear old Belle, she has long been dreaming among the lotus-flowers and poppies of the dogs' paradise.

Certain dreams have haunted me since my childhood. One which recurs often proceeds after this wise: A spirit seems to pass before my face. I feel an extreme heat like the blast from an engine. It is the embodiment of evil. I must have had it first after the day that I nearly got burnt.

Another spirit which visits me often brings a sensation of cool dampness, such as one feels on a chill November night when the window is open. The spirit stops just beyond my reach, sways back and forth like a creature in grief. My blood is chilled, and seems to freeze in my veins. I try to move, but my body is still, and I cannot even cry out. After a while the spirit passes on, and I say to myself shudderingly, "That was Death. I wonder if he has taken her." The pronoun stands for my Teacher.

In my dreams I have sensations, odors, tastes and ideas which I do not remember to have had in reality. Perhaps they are the glimpses which my mind catches through the veil of sleep of my earliest babyhood. I have heard "the trampling of many waters." Sometimes a wonderful light visits me in sleep. Such a flash and glory as it is! I gaze and gaze until it vanishes. I smell and taste much as in my waking hours; but the sense of touch plays a less important part. In sleep I almost never grope. No one guides me. Even in a crowded street I am self-sufficient, and I enjoy an independence quite foreign to my physical life. Now I seldom spell on my fingers, and it is still rarer for others to spell into my hand. My mind acts independent of my physical organs. I am delighted to be thus endowed, if only in sleep; for then my soul dons its winged sandals and joyfully joins the throng of happy beings who dwell beyond the reaches of bodily sense.

The moral inconsistency of dreams is glaring. Mine grow less and less accordant with my proper principles. I am nightly hurled into an unethical medley of extremes. I must either defend another to the last drop of my blood or condemn him past all repenting. I commit murder, sleeping, to save the lives of others. I ascribe to those I love best acts and words which it mortifies me to remember, and I cast reproach after reproach upon them. It is fortunate for our peace of mind that most wicked dreams are soon forgotten. Death, sudden and awful, strange loves and hates remorselessly pursued, cunningly plotted revenge, are seldom more than dim haunting recollections in the morning, and during the day they are erased by the normal activities of the mind. Sometimes immediately on waking, I am so vexed at the memory of a dream-fracas, I wish I may dream no more. With this wish distinctly before me I drop off again into a new turmoil of dreams.

Oh, dreams, what opprobrium I heap upon you—you, the most pointless things imaginable, saucy apes, brewers of odious contrasts, haunting birds of ill omen, mocking echoes, unseasonable reminders, oft-returning vexations, skeletons in my morris-chair, jesters in the tomb, death's-heads at the wedding feast, outlaws of the brain that every night defy the mind's police service, thieves of my Hesperidean apples, breakers of my domestic peace, murderers of sleep. "Oh, dreadful dreams that do fright my spirit from her propriety!" No wonder that

Hamlet preferred the ills he knew rather than run the risk of one dream-vision.

Yet remove the dream-world, and the loss is inconceivable. The magic spell which binds poetry together is broken. The splendor of art and the soaring might of imagination are lessened because no phantom of fadeless sunsets and flowers urges onward to a goal. Gone is the mute permission or connivance which emboldens the soul to mock the limits of time and space, forecast and gather in harvests of achievement for ages yet unborn. Blot out dreams, and the blind lose one of their chief comforts; for in the visions of sleep they behold their belief in the seeing mind and their expectation of light beyond the blank, narrow night justified. Nay, our conception of immortality is shaken. Faith, the motive-power of human life, flickers out. Before such vacancy and bareness the shock of wrecked worlds were indeed welcome. In truth, dreams bring us the thought independently of us and in spite of us that the soul

                              may right
        Her nature, shoot large sail on lengthening cord,
        And rush exultant on the Infinite.

XIV. Dreams and Reality

IT is astonishing to think how our real wide-awake life revolves around the shadowy unrealities of Dreamland. Despite all that we say about the inconsequence of dreams, we often reason by them. We stake our greatest hopes upon them. Nay, we build upon them the fabric of an ideal world. I can recall few fine, thoughtful poems, few noble works of art or any system of philosophy in which there is not evidence that dream-fantasies symbolize truths concealed by phenomena.

The fact that in dreams confusion reigns, and illogical connections occur gives plausibility to the theory which Sir Arthur Mitchell and other scientific men hold, that our dream-thinking is uncontrolled and undirected by the will. The will—the inhibiting and guiding power—finds rest and refreshment in sleep, while the mind, like a barque without rudder or compass, drifts aimlessly upon an uncharted sea. But curiously enough, these fantasies and inter-twistings of thought are to be found in great imaginative poems like Spenser's "Færie Queene." Lamb was impressed by the analogy between our dream-thinking and the work of the imagination. Speaking of the episode in the cave of Mammon, Lamb wrote:

"It is not enough to say that the whole episode is a copy of the mind's conceptions in sleep; it is—in some sort, but what a copy! Let the most romantic of us that has been entertained all night with the spectacle of some wild and magnificent vision, re-combine it in the morning and try it by his waking judgment. That which appeared so shifting and yet so coherent, when that faculty was passive, when it comes under cool examination, shall appear so reasonless and so unlinked, that we are ashamed to have been so deluded, and to have taken, though but in sleep, a monster for a god. But the transitions in this episode are every whit as violent as in the most extravagant dream, and yet the waking judgment ratifies them."

Perhaps I feel more than others the analogy between the world of our waking life and the world of dreams because before I was taught, I lived in a sort of perpetual dream. The testimony of parents and friends who watched me day after day is the only means that I have of knowing the actuality of those early, obscure years of my childhood. The physical acts of going to bed and waking in the morning alone mark the transition from reality to Dreamland. As near as I can tell, asleep or awake I only felt with my body. I can recollect no process which I should now dignify with the term of thought. It is true that my bodily sensations were extremely acute; but beyond a crude connection with physical wants they are not associated or directed. They had little relation to each other, to me, or to the experience of others. Idea—that which gives identity and continuity to experience—came into my sleeping and waking existence at the same moment with the awakening of self-consciousness. Before that moment my mind was in a state of anarchy in which meaningless sensations rioted, and if thought existed, it was so vague and inconsequent, it cannot be made a part of discourse. Yet before my education began, I dreamed. I know that I must have dreamed because I recall no break in my tactual experiences. Things fell suddenly, heavily. I felt my clothing afire, or I fell into a tub of cold water. Once I smelt bananas, and the odor in my nostrils was so vivid that in the morning, before I was dressed, I went to the sideboard to look for the bananas. There were no bananas, and no odor of bananas anywhere! My life was in fact a dream throughout.

The likeness between my waking state and the sleeping one is still marked. In both states I see, but not with my eyes. I hear, but not with my ears. I speak, and am spoken to, without the sound of a voice. I am moved to pleasure by visions of ineffable beauty which I have never beheld in the physical world. Once in a dream I held in my hand a pearl. I have no memory-vision of a real pearl. The one I saw in my dreams must, therefore, have been a creation of my imagination. It was a smooth, exquisitely molded crystal. As I gazed into its shimmering deeps, my soul was flooded with an ecstasy of tenderness, and I was filled with wonder as one who should for the first time look into the cool, sweet heart of a rose. My pearl was dew and fire, the velvety green of moss, the soft whiteness of lilies, and the distilled hues and sweetness of a thousand roses. It seemed to me, the soul of beauty was dissolved in its crystal bosom. This beauteous vision strengthens my conviction that the world which the mind builds up out of countless subtle experiences and suggestions is fairer than the world of the senses. The splendor of the sunset my friends gaze at across the purpling hills is wonderful. But the sunset of the inner vision brings purer delight because it is the worshipful blending of all the beauty that we have known and desired.

I believe that I am more fortunate in my dreams than most people; for as I think back over my dreams, the pleasant ones seem to predominate, although we naturally recall most vividly and tell most eagerly the grotesque and fantastic adventures in Slumberland. I have friends, however, whose dreams are always troubled and disturbed. They wake fatigued and bruised, and they tell me that they would give a kingdom for one dreamless night. There is one friend who declares that she has never had a felicitous dream in her life. The grind and worry of the day invade the sweet domain of sleep and weary her with incessant, profitless effort. I feel very sorry for this friend, and perhaps it is hardly fair to insist upon the pleasure of dreaming in the presence of one whose dream-experience is so unhappy. Still, it is true that my dreams have uses as many and sweet as those of adversity. All my yearning for the strange, the weird, the ghost-like is gratified in dreams. They carry me out of the accustomed and commonplace. In a flash, in the winking of an eye they snatch the burden from my shoulder, the trivial task from my hand and the pain and disappointment from my heart, and I behold the lovely face of my dream. It dances round me with merry measure and darts hither and thither in happy abandon. Sudden, sweet fancies spring forth from every nook and corner, and delightful surprises meet me at every turn. A happy dream is more precious than gold and rubies.

I like to think that in dreams we catch glimpses of a life larger than our own. We see it as a little child, or as a savage who visits a civilized nation. Thoughts are imparted to us far above our ordinary thinking. Feelings nobler and wiser than any we have known thrill us between heart-beats. For one fleeting night a princelier nature captures us, and we become as great as our aspirations. I daresay we return to the little world of our daily activities with as distorted a half-memory of what we have seen as that of the African who visited England, and afterwards said he had been in a huge hill which carried him over great waters. The comprehensiveness of our thought, whether we are asleep or awake, no doubt depends largely upon our idiosyncrasies, constitution, habits, and mental capacity. But whatever may be the nature of our dreams, the mental processes that characterize them are analogous to those which go on when the mind is not held to attention by the will.

XV. A Waking Dream

I HAVE sat for hours in a sort of reverie, letting my mind have its way without inhibition and direction, and idly noted down the incessant beat of thought upon thought, image upon image. I have observed that my thoughts make all kinds of connections, wind in and out, trace concentric circles, and break up in eddies of fantasy, just as in dreams. One day I had a literary frolic with a certain set of thoughts which dropped in for an afternoon call. I wrote for three or four hours as they arrived, and the resulting record is much like a dream. I found that the most disconnected, dissimilar thoughts came in arm-in-arm—I dreamed a wide-awake dream. The difference is that in waking dreams I can look back upon the endless succession of thoughts, while in the dreams of sleep I can recall but few ideas and images. I catch broken threads from the warp and woof of a pattern I cannot see, or glowing leaves which have floated on a slumber-wind from a tree that I cannot identify. In this reverie I held the key to the company of ideas. I give my record of them to show what analogies exist between thoughts when they are not directed and the behaviour of real dream-thinking.

I had an essay to write. I wanted my mind fresh and obedient, and all its handmaidens ready to hold up my hands in the task. I intended to discourse learnedly upon my educational experiences, and I was unusually anxious to do my best. I had a working plan in my head for the essay, which was to be grave, wise, and abounding in ideas. Moreover, it was to have an academic flavor suggestive of sheepskin, and the reader was to be duly impressed with the austere dignity of cap and gown. I shut myself up in the study, resolved to beat out on the keys of my typewriter this immortal chapter of my life-history. Alexander was no more confident of conquering Asia with the splendid army which his father Philip had disciplined than I was of finding my mental house in order and my thoughts obedient. My mind had had a long vacation, and I was now coming back to it in an hour that it looked not for me. My situation was similar to that of the master who went into a far country and expected on his home coming to find everything as he left it. But returning he found his servants giving a party. Confusion was rampant. There was fiddling and dancing and the babble of many tongues, so that the voice of the master could not be heard. Though he shouted and beat upon the gate, it remained closed.

So it was with me. I sounded the trumpet loud and long; but the vassals of thought would not rally to my standard. Each had his arm round the waist of a fair partner, and I know not what wild tunes "put life and mettle into their heels." There was nothing to do. I looked about helplessly upon my great retinue, and realized that it is not the possession of a thing but the ability to use it which is of value. I settled back in my chair to watch the pageant. It was rather pleasant sitting there, "idle as a painted ship upon a painted ocean," watching my own thoughts at play. It was like thinking fine things to say without taking the trouble to write them. I felt like Alice in Wonderland when she ran at full speed with the red queen and never passed anything or got anywhere.

The merry frolic went on madly. The dancers were all manner of thoughts. There were sad thoughts and happy thoughts, thoughts suited to every clime and weather, thoughts bearing the mark of every age and nation, silly thoughts and wise thoughts, thoughts of people, of things, and of nothing, good thoughts, impish thoughts and large, gracious thoughts. There they went swinging hand-in-hand in corkscrew fashion. An antic jester in green and gold led the dance. The guests followed no order or precedent. No two thoughts were related to each other even by

the fortieth cousinship. There was not so much as an international
alliance between them. Each thought behaved like a newly created poet.

> His mouth he could not ope,
> But there flew out a trope.

Magical lyrics—oh, if I only had written them down! Pell-
mell they came down the sequestered avenues of my mind, this
merry throng. With bacchanal song and shout they came, and
eye hath not since beheld confusion worse confounded.

Shut your eyes, and see them come—the knights and ladies
of my revel. Plumed and turbaned they come, clad in mail and
silken broideries, gentle maids in Quaker gray, gay princes in
scarlet cloaks, coquettes with roses in their hair, monks in cowls
that might have covered the tall Minster Tower, demure little
girls hugging paper dolls, and rollicking school-boys with ruddy
morning faces, an absent-minded professor carrying his shoes
under his arms and looking wise, followed by cronies, fairies,
goblins, and all the troops just loosed from Noah's storm-tossed
ark. They walked, they strutted, they soared, they swam, and
some came in through fire. One sprite climbed up to the moon
on a ladder made of leaves and frozen dew-drops. A peacock
with a great hooked bill flew in and out among the branches of
a pomegranate-tree pecking the rosy fruit. He screamed so loud
that Apollo turned in his chariot of flame and from his burnished
bow shot golden arrows at him. This did not disturb the peacock
in the least; for he spread his gem-like wings and flourished
his wonderful, fire-tipped tail in the very face of the sun-god!
Then came Venus—an exact copy of my own plaster cast—
serene, calm-eyed, dancing "high and disposedly" like Queen
Elizabeth, surrounded by a troop of lovely Cupids mounted on
rose-tinted clouds, blown hither and thither by sweet winds,
while all around danced flowers and streams and queer little
Japanese cherry-trees in pots! They were followed by jovial Pan
with green hair and jeweled sandals, and by his side—I could
scarcely believe my eyes!—walked a modest nun counting her
beads. At a little distance were seen three dancers arm-in-arm,

The Little Boy Next Door

a lean, starved platitude, a rosy, dimpled joke, and a steel-ribbed sermon on predestination. Close upon them came a whole string of Nights with wind-blown hair and Days with fagots on their backs. All at once I saw the ample figure of Life rise above the whirling mass holding a naked child in one hand and in the other a gleaming sword. A bear crouched at her feet, and all about her swirled and glowed a multitudinous host of tiny atoms which sang all together, "We are the will of God." Atom wedded atom, and chemical married chemical, and the cosmic dance went on in changing, changeless measure, until my head sang like a buzz-saw.

Just as I was thinking I would leave this scene of phantoms and take a stroll in the quiet groves of Slumber I noticed a commotion near one of the entrances to my enchanted palace. It was evident from the whispering and buzzing that went round that more celebrities had arrived. The first personage I saw was Homer, blind no more, leading by a golden chain the white-beaked ships of the Achaians bobbing their heads and squawking like so many white swans. Plato and Mother Goose with the numerous children of the shoe came next. Simple Simon, Jill and Jack, who had just had his head mended, and the cat that fell into the cream—all these danced in a giddy reel, while Plato solemnly discoursed on the laws of Topsyturvy Land. Then followed grim-visaged Calvin and "violet-crowned, sweet-smiling Sappho" who danced a Schottische. Aristophanes and Molière joined for a measure, both talking at once, Molière in Greek and Aristophanes in German. I thought this odd because it occurred to me that German was a dead language before Aristophanes was born. Bright-eyed Shelley brought in a fluttering lark which burst into the song of Chaucer's chanticleer. Henry Esmond gave his hand in a stately minuet to Diana of the Crossways. He evidently did not understand her nineteenth-century wit; for he did not laugh. Perhaps he had lost his taste for clever women. Anon Dante and Swedenborg came together conversing earnestly about things remote and mystical. Swedenborg said it was very warm. Dante replied that it might rain in the night.

Suddenly there was a great clamor, and I found that "The Battle of the Books" had begun raging anew. Two figures entered in lively dispute. One was dressed in plain homespun and the other wore a scholar's gown over a suit of motley. I gathered from their conversation that they were Cotton Mather and William Shakespeare. Mather insisted that the witches in "Macbeth" should be caught and hanged. Shakespeare replied that the witches had already suffered enough at the hands of commentators. They were pushed aside by the twelve knights of the Round Table, who marched in bearing on a salver the goose that laid golden eggs. "The Pope's Mule" and "The Golden Bull" had a combat of history and fiction such as I had read of in books, but never before witnessed. These little animals were put to rout by a huge elephant which lumbered in with Rudyard Kipling riding high on its trunk. The elephant changed suddenly to "a rakish craft." (I do not know what a rakish craft is; but this was very rakish and very crafty.) It must have been abandoned long ago by wild pirates of the southern seas; for clinging to the rigging, and jovially cheering as the ship went down, I made out a man with blazing eyes, clad in a velveteen jacket. As the ship disappeared from sight, Falstaff rushed to the rescue of the lonely navigator—and stole his purse! But Miranda persuaded him to give it back. Stevenson said, "Who steals my purse steals trash." Falstaff laughed and called this a good joke, as good as any he had heard in his day.

This was the signal for a rushing swarm of quotations. They surged to and fro, an inchoate throng of half-finished phrases, mutilated sentences, parodied sentiments, and brilliant metaphors. I could not distinguish any phrases or ideas of my own making. I saw a poor, ragged, shrunken sentence that might have been mine own catch the wings of a fair idea with the light of genius shining like a halo about its head.

Ever and anon the dancers changed partners without invitation or permission. Thoughts fell in love at sight, married in a measure, and joined hands without previous courtship. An incongruity is the wedding of two thoughts which have had no reasonable courtship, and marriages without wooing are apt to lead to domestic discord, even to the breaking up of an ancient, time-honoured family. Among the wedded couples were certain similes hitherto inviolable in their bachelorhood and spinster-hood, and held in great respect. Their extraordinary proceedings nearly broke up the dance. But the fatuity of their union was evident to them, and they parted. Other similes seemed to have the habit of living in discord. They had been many times married and divorced. They belonged to the notorious society of Mixed Metaphors.

A company of phantoms floated in and out wearing tan-talizing garments of oblivion. They seemed about to dance, then vanished. They reappeared half a dozen times, but never unveiled their faces. The imp Curiosity pulled Memory by the sleeve and said, "Why do they run away? 'T is strange knav-ery!" Out ran Memory to capture them. After a great deal of racing and puffing and collision it apprehended some of the fugitives and brought them in. But when it tore off their masks, lo! some were disappointingly commonplace, and others were gipsy quotations trying to conceal the punctuation marks that belonged to them. Memory was much chagrined to have had such a hard chase only to catch this sorry lot of graceless rogues.

Into the rabble strode four stately giants who called them-selves History, Philosophy, Law, and Medicine. They seemed too solemn and imposing to join in a masque. But even as I gazed at these formidable guests, they all split into fragments which went whirling, dancing in divisions, subdivisions, re-subdivisions of scientific nonsense! History split into philology, ethnology, anthropology, and mythology, and these again split finer than the splitting of hairs. Each speciality hugged its bit of knowl-edge and waltzed it round and round. The rest of the company began to nod, and I felt drowsy myself. To put an end to the solemn gyrations, a troop of fairies mercifully waved poppies over us all, the masque faded, my head fell, and I started. Sleep had wakened me. At my elbow I found my old friend Bottom.

"Bottom," I said, "I have had a dream past the wit of man to say what dream it was. Methought I was—there is no man can tell what. The eye of man hath not heard, the ear of man hath not seen, his hand is not able to taste, his tongue to conceive, nor his heart to report what my dream was."

A Chant of Darkness

"My wings are folded o'er mine ears,
My wings are crossèd o'er mine eyes,
Yet through their silver shade appears,
And through their lulling plumes arise,
A Shape, a throng of sounds."
                    Shelley's *"Prometheus Unbound."*

I

I dare not ask why we are reft of light,
Banished to our solitary isles amid the unmeasured seas,
Or how our sight was nurtured to glorious vision,
To fade and vanish and leave us in the dark alone.
The secret of God is upon our tabernacle;
Into His mystery I dare not pry. Only this I know:
With Him is strength, with Him is wisdom,
And His wisdom hath set darkness in our paths.
Out of the uncharted, unthinkable dark we came,
And in a little time we shall return again
Into the vast, unanswering dark.

O Dark! thou awful, sweet, and holy Dark!
In thy solemn spaces, beyond the human eye,
God fashioned His universe; laid the foundations of the earth,
Laid the measure thereof, and stretched the line upon it;
Shut up the sea with doors, and made the glory
Of the clouds a covering for it;
Commanded His morning, and, behold! chaos fled

Before the uplifted face of the sun;
Divided a water-course for the overflowing of waters;
Sent rain upon the earth—
Upon the wilderness wherein there was no man,
Upon the desert where grew no tender herb,
And, lo! there was greenness upon the plains,
And the hills were clothed with beauty!
Out of the uncharted, unthinkable dark we came,
And in a little time we shall return again
Into the vast, unanswering dark.

O Dark! thou secret and inscrutable Dark!
In thy silent depths, the springs whereof man hath not
    fathomed,
God wrought the soul of man.
O Dark! compassionate, all-knowing Dark!
Tenderly, as shadows to the evening, comes thy message to man.
Softly thou layest thy hand on his tired eyelids,
And his soul, weary and homesick, returns
Unto thy soothing embrace.
Out of the uncharted, unthinkable dark we came,
And in a little time we shall return again
Into the vast, unanswering dark.

O Dark! wise, vital, thought-quickening Dark!
In thy mystery thou hidest the light
That is the soul's life.
Upon thy solitary shores I walk unafraid;
I dread no evil; though I walk in the valley of the shadow,
I shall not know the ecstasy of fear
When gentle Death leads me through life's open door,
When the bands of night are sundered,
And the day outpours its light.
Out of the uncharted, unthinkable dark we came,
And in a little time we shall return again
Into the vast, unanswering dark.

The timid soul, fear-driven, shuns the dark;
But upon the cheeks of him who must abide in shadow
Breathes the wind of rushing angel-wings,
And round him falls a light from unseen fires.

Magical beams glow athwart the darkness;
Paths of beauty wind through his black world
To another world of light,
Where no veil of sense shuts him out from Paradise.
Out of the uncharted, unthinkable dark we came,
And in a little time we shall return again
Into the vast, unanswering dark.

O Dark! thou blessèd, quiet Dark!
To the lone exile who must dwell with thee
Thou art benign and friendly;
From the harsh world thou dost shut him in;
To him thou whisperest the secrets of the wondrous night;
Upon him thou bestowest regions wide and boundless as his
    spirit;
Thou givest a glory to all humble things;
With thy hovering pinions thou coverest all unlovely objects;
Under thy brooding wings there is peace.
Out of the uncharted, unthinkable dark we came,
And in a little time we shall return again
Into the vast, unanswering dark.

II

Once in regions void of light I wandered;
In blank darkness I stumbled,
And fear led me by the hand;
My feet pressed earthward,
Afraid of pitfalls.
By many shapeless terrors of the night affrighted,
To the wakeful day
I held out beseeching arms.

Then came Love, bearing in her hand
The torch that is the light unto my feet,
And softly spoke Love: "Hast thou
Entered into the treasures of darkness?
Hast thou entered into the treasures of the night?

Search out thy blindness. It holdeth
Riches past computing."

The words of Love set my spirit aflame.
My eager fingers searched out the mysteries,
The splendors, the inmost sacredness, of things,
And in the vacancies discerned
With spiritual sense the fullness of life;
And the gates of Day stood wide.

I am shaken with gladness;
My limbs tremble with joy;
My heart and the earth
Tremble with happiness;
The ecstasy of life
Is abroad in the world.

Knowledge hath uncurtained heaven;
On the uttermost shores of darkness there is light;
Midnight hath sent forth a beam!
The blind that stumbled in darkness without light
Behold a new day!
In the obscurity gleams the star of Thought;
Imagination hath a luminous eye,
And the mind hath a glorious vision.

III

"The man is blind. What is life to him?
A closed book held up against a sightless face.
Would that he could see
Yon beauteous star, and know
For one transcendent moment
The palpitating joy of sight!"

All sight is of the soul.
Behold it in the upward flight
Of the unfettered spirit! Hast thou seen

Thought bloom in the blind child's face?
Hast thou seen his mind grow,
Like the running dawn, to grasp
The vision of the Master?
It was the miracle of inward sight.

In the realms of wonderment where I dwell
I explore life with my hands;
I recognize, and am happy;
My fingers are ever athirst for the earth,
And drink up its wonders with delight,
Draw out earth's dear delights;
My feet are charged with the murmur,
The throb, of all things that grow.

This is touch, this quivering,
This flame, this ether,
This glad rush of blood,
This daylight in my heart,
This glow of sympathy in my palms!
Thou blind, loving, all-prying touch,
Thou openest the book of life to me.
The noiseless little noises of the earth
Come with softest rustle;
The shy, sweet feet of life;
The silky mutter of moth-wings
Against my restraining palm;
The strident beat of insect-wings,
The silvery trickle of water;
Little breezes busy in the summer grass;
The music of crisp, whisking, scurrying leaves,
The swirling, wind-swept, frost-tinted leaves;
The crystal splash of summer rain,
Saturate with the odors of the sod.

With alert fingers I listen
To the showers of sound
That the wind shakes from the forest.
I bathe in the liquid shade
Under the pines, where the air hangs cool
After the shower is done.

My saucy little friend the squirrel
Flips my shoulder with his tail,
Leaps from leafy billow to leafy billow,
Returns to eat his breakfast from my hand.
Between us there is glad sympathy;
He gambols; my pulses dance;
I am exultingly full of the joy of life!

Have not my fingers split the sand
On the sun-flooded beach?
Hath not my naked body felt the water sing
When the sea hath enveloped it
With rippling music?
Have I not felt
The lilt of waves beneath my boat,
The flap of sail,
The strain of mast,
The wild rush
Of the lightning-charged winds?
Have I not smelt the swift, keen flight
Of winged odors before the tempest?
Here is joy awake, aglow;
Here is the tumult of the heart.

My hands evoke sight and sound out of feeling,
Intershifting the senses endlessly;
Linking motion with sight, odor with sound
They give color to the honeyed breeze,
The measure and passion of a symphony
To the beat and quiver of unseen wings.
In the secrets of earth and sun and air
My fingers are wise;
They snatch light out of darkness,
They thrill to harmonies breathed in silence.

I walked in the stillness of the night,
And my soul uttered her gladness.
O Night, still, odorous Night, I love thee!
O wide, spacious Night, I love thee!
O steadfast, glorious Night!
I touch thee with my hands;

I lean against thy strength;
I am comforted.

O fathomless, soothing Night!
Thou art a balm to my restless spirit,
I nestle gratefully in thy bosom,
Dark, gracious mother!
Like a dove, I rest in thy bosom.
Out of the uncharted, unthinkable dark we came,
And in a little time we shall return again
Into the vast, unanswering dark.

Helen Keller

Part I. Optimism Within

COULD we choose our environment, and were desire in human undertakings synonymous with endowment, all men would, I suppose, be optimists. Certainly most of us regard happiness as the proper end of all earthly enterprise. The will to be happy animates alike the philosopher, the prince and the chimney-sweep. No matter how dull, or how mean, or how wise a man is, he feels that happiness is his indisputable right.

It is curious to observe what different ideals of happiness people cherish, and in what singular places they look for this well-spring of their life. Many look for it in the hoarding of riches, some in the pride of power, and others in the achievements of art and literature; a few seek it in the exploration of their own minds, or in the search for knowledge.

Most people measure their happiness in terms of physical pleasure and material possession. Could they win some visible goal which they have set on the horizon, how happy they would be! Lacking this gift or that circumstance, they would be miserable. If happiness is to be so measured, I who cannot hear or see have every reason to sit in a corner with folded hands and weep. If I am happy in spite of my deprivations, if my happiness is so deep that it is a faith, so thoughtful that it becomes a philosophy of life,—if, in short, I am an optimist, my testimony to the creed of optimism is worth hearing. As sinners stand up in meeting and testify to the goodness of God, so one who is called afflicted may rise up in gladness of conviction and testify to the goodness of life.

Once I knew the depth where no hope was, and darkness lay on the face of all things. Then love came and set my soul free.

Once I knew only darkness and stillness. Now I know hope and joy. Once I fretted and beat myself against the wall that shut me in. Now I rejoice in the consciousness that I can think, act and attain heaven. My life was without past or future; death, the pessimist would say, "a consummation devoutly to be wished." But a little word from the fingers of another fell into my hand that clutched at emptiness, and my heart leaped to the rapture of living. Night fled before the day of thought, and love and joy and hope came up in a passion of obedience to knowledge. Can any one who has escaped such captivity, who has felt the thrill and glory of freedom, be a pessimist?

My early experience was thus a leap from bad to good. If I tried, I could not check the momentum of my first leap out of the dark; to move breast forward is a habit learned suddenly at that first moment of release and rush into the light. With the first word I used intelligently, I learned to live, to think, to hope. Darkness cannot shut me in again. I have had a glimpse of the shore, and can now live by the hope of reaching it.

So my optimism is no mild and unreasoning satisfaction. A poet once said I must be happy because I did not see the bare, cold present, but lived in a beautiful dream. I do live in a beautiful dream; but that dream is the actual, the present—not cold, but warm; not bare, but furnished with a thousand blessings. The very evil which the poet supposed would be a cruel disillusionment is necessary to the fullest knowledge of joy. Only by contact with evil could I have learned to feel by contrast the beauty of truth and love and goodness.

It is a mistake always to contemplate the good and ignore the evil, because by making people neglectful it lets in disaster. There is a dangerous optimism of ignorance and indifference. It is not enough to say that the twentieth century is the best age in the history of mankind, and to take refuge from the evils of the world in skyey dreams of good. How many good men, prosperous and contented, looked around and saw naught but good, while millions of their fellowmen were bartered and sold like cattle! No doubt, there were comfortable optimists who thought Wilberforce a meddlesome fanatic when he was working with

might and main to free the slaves. I distrust the rash optimism
in this country that cries, "Hurrah, we're all right! This is the
greatest nation on earth," when there are grievances that call
loudly for redress. That is false optimism. Optimism that does
not count the cost is like a house builded on sand. A man must
understand evil and be acquainted with sorrow before he can
write himself an optimist and expect others to believe that he
has reason for the faith that is in him.

I know what evil is. Once or twice I have wrestled with it,
and for a time felt its chilling touch on my life; so I speak with
knowledge when I say that evil is of no consequence, except
as a sort of mental gymnastic. For the very reason that I have
come in contact with it, I am more truly an optimist. I can say
with conviction that the struggle which evil necessitates is one of
the greatest blessings. It makes us strong, patient, helpful men
and women. It lets us into the soul of things and teaches us that
although the world is full of suffering, it is full also of the over-
coming of it. My optimism, then, does not rest on the absence
of evil, but on a glad belief in the preponderance of good and
a willing effort always to coöperate with the good, that it may
prevail. I try to increase the power God has given me to see the
best in everything and every one, and make that Best a part of
my life. The world is sown with good; but unless I turn my glad
thoughts into practical living and till my own field, I cannot reap
a kernel of the good.

Thus my optimism is grounded in two worlds, myself and
what is about me. I demand that the world be good, and lo, it
obeys. I proclaim the world good, and facts range themselves to
prove my proclamation overwhelmingly true. To what is good
I open the doors of my being, and jealously shut them against
what is bad. Such is the force of this beautiful and wilful conviction, it carries itself in the face of all opposition. I am never
discouraged by absence of good. I never can be argued into
hopelessness. Doubt and mistrust are the mere panic of timid
imagination, which the steadfast heart will conquer, and the
large mind transcend.

As my college days draw to a close, I find myself looking

forward with beating heart and bright anticipations to what the future holds of activity for me. My share in the work of the world may be limited; but the fact that it is work makes it precious. Nay, the desire and will to work is optimism itself.

Two generations ago Carlyle flung forth his gospel of work. To the dreamers of the Revolution, who built cloud-castles of happiness, and, when the inevitable winds rent the castles asunder, turned pessimists—to those ineffectual Endymions, Alastors and Werthers, this Scots peasant, man of dreams in the hard, practical world, cried aloud his creed of labor. "Be no longer a Chaos, but a World. Produce! produce! Were it but the pitifullest infinitesimal fraction of a product, produce it, in God's name! 'T is the utmost thou hast in thee; out with it, then. Up, up! whatsoever thy hand findeth to do, do it with thy whole might. Work while it is called To-day; for the Night cometh wherein no man may work."

Some have said Carlyle was taking refuge from a hard world by bidding men grind and toil, eyes to the earth, and so forget their misery. This is not Carlyle's thought. "Fool!" he cries, "the Ideal is in thyself; the Impediment is also in thyself. Work out the Ideal in the poor, miserable Actual; live, think, believe, and be free!" It is plain what he says, that work, production, brings life out of chaos, makes the individual a world, an order; and order is optimism.

I, too, can work, and because I love to labor with my head and my hands, I am an optimist in spite of all. I used to think I should be thwarted in my desire to do something useful. But I have found out that though the ways in which I can make myself useful are few, yet the work open to me is endless. The gladdest laborer in the vineyard may be a cripple. Even should the others outstrip him, yet the vineyard ripens in the sun each year, and the full clusters weigh into his hand. Darwin could work only half an hour at a time; yet in many diligent half-hours he laid anew the foundations of philosophy. I long to accomplish a great and noble task; but it is my chief duty and joy to accomplish humble tasks as though they were great and noble. It is my service to think how I can best fulfil the demands that each day makes upon me, and to rejoice that others can do what I cannot. Green, the historian,[1] tells us that the world is moved along, not only by the mighty shoves of its heroes, but also by the aggregate of the tiny pushes of each honest worker; and that thought alone suffices to guide me in this dark world and wide. I love the good that others do; for their activity is an assurance that whether I can help or not, the true and the good will stand sure.

I trust, and nothing that happens disturbs my trust. I recognize the beneficence of the power which we all worship as supreme—Order, Fate, the Great Spirit, Nature, God. I recognize this power in the sun that makes all things grow and keeps life afoot. I make a friend of this indefinable force, and straightway I feel glad, brave and ready for any lot Heaven may decree for me. This is my religion of optimism.

---

[1] Life and Letters of John Richard Green. Edited by Leslie Stephen.

Part II. Optimism Without

OPTIMISM, then, is a fact within my own heart. But as I look out upon life, my heart meets no contradiction. The outward world justifies my inward universe of good. All through the years I have spent in college, my reading has been a continuous discovery of good. In literature, philosophy, religion and history I find the mighty witnesses to my faith.

Philosophy is the history of a deaf-blind person writ large. From the talks of Socrates up through Plato, Berkeley and Kant, philosophy records the efforts of human intelligence to be free of the clogging material world and fly forth into a universe of pure idea. A deaf-blind person ought to find special meaning in Plato's Ideal World. These things which you see and hear and touch are not the reality of realities, but imperfect manifestations of the Idea, the Principle, the Spiritual; the Idea is the truth, the rest is delusion.

If this be so, my brethren who enjoy the fullest use of the senses are not aware of any reality which may not equally well be in reach of my mind. Philosophy gives to the mind the prerogative of seeing truth, and bears us into a realm where I, who am blind, am not different from you who see. When I learned from Berkeley that your eyes receive an inverted image of things which your brain unconsciously corrects, I began to suspect that the eye is not a very reliable instrument after all, and I felt as one who had been restored to equality with others, glad, not because the senses avail them so little, but because in God's eternal world, mind and spirit avail so much. It seemed to me that philosophy had been written for my special consolation, whereby I get even with some modern philosophers who apparently think that I was intended as an experimental case for their special instruction! But in a little measure my small voice of individual experience does join in the declaration of philosophy that the good is the only world, and that world is a world of spirit. It is also a universe where order is All, where an unbroken logic holds the parts together, where disorder defines itself as non-existence, where evil, as St. Augustine held, is delusion, and therefore is not.

The meaning of philosophy to me is not only in its principles, but also in the happy isolation of its great expounders. They were seldom of the world, even when like Plato and Leibnitz they moved in its courts and drawing-rooms. To the tumult of life they were deaf, and they were blind to its distraction and perplexing diversities. Sitting alone, but not in darkness, they learned to find everything in themselves, and failing to find it even there, they still trusted in meeting the truth face to face when they should leave the earth behind and become partakers in the wisdom of God. The great mystics lived alone, deaf and blind, but dwelling with God.

I understand how it was possible for Spinoza to find deep and sustained happiness when he was excommunicated, poor, despised and suspected alike by Jew and Christian; not that the kind world of men ever treated me so, but that his isolation from the universe of sensuous joys is somewhat analogous to mine. He loved the good for its own sake. Like many great spirits he accepted his place in the world, and confided himself childlike to a higher power, believing that it worked through his hands and predominated in his being. He trusted implicitly, and that is what I do. Deep, solemn optimism, it seems to me, should spring from this firm belief in the presence of God in the individual; not a remote, unapproachable governor of the universe, but a God who is very near every one of us, who is present not only in earth, sea and sky, but also in every pure and noble impulse of our hearts, "the source and centre of all minds, their only point of rest."

Thus from philosophy I learn that we see only shadows and know only in part, and that all things change; but the mind, the unconquerable mind, compasses all truth, embraces the universe as it is, converts the shadows to realities and makes tumultuous changes seem but moments in an eternal silence, or short lines in the infinite theme of perfection, and the evil but "a halt on the way to good." Though with my hand I grasp only a small part of the universe, with my spirit I see the whole, and in my thought I can compass the beneficent laws by which it is governed. The confidence and trust which these conceptions inspire teach me to rest safe in my life as in a fate, and protect me from spectral doubts and fears. Verily, blessed are ye that have not seen, and yet have believed.

All the world's great philosophers have been lovers of God and believers in man's inner goodness. To know the history of philosophy is to know that the highest thinkers of the ages, the seers of the tribes and the nations, have been optimists.

The growth of philosophy is the story of man's spiritual life. Outside lies that great mass of events which we call History. As I look on this mass, I see it take form and shape itself in the ways of God. The history of man is an epic of progress. In the world within and the world without I see a wonderful correspondence, a glorious symbolism which reveals the human and the divine communing together, the lesson of philosophy repeated in fact. In all the parts that compose the history of mankind hides the spirit of good, and gives meaning to the whole.

Far back in the twilight of history I see the savage fleeing from the forces of nature which he has not learned to control, and seeking to propitiate supernatural beings which are but the creation of his superstitious fear. With a shift of imagination I see the savage emancipated, civilized. He no longer worships the grim deities of ignorance. Through suffering he has learned to build a roof over his head, to defend his life and his home, and over his state he has erected a temple in which he worships the joyous gods of light and song. From suffering he has learned justice; from the struggle with his fellows he has learned the distinction between right and wrong which makes him a moral being. He is gifted with the genius of Greece.

But Greece was not perfect. Her poetical and religious ideals were far above her practice; therefore she died, that her ideals might survive to ennoble coming ages.

Rome, too, left the world a rich inheritance. Through the vicissitudes of history her laws and ordered government have stood a majestic object-lesson for the ages. But when the stern, frugal character of her people ceased to be the bone and sinew of her civilization, Rome fell.

Then came the new nations of the North and founded a more permanent society. The base of Greek and Roman society was the slave, crushed into the condition of the wretches who "labored, foredone, in the field and at the workshop, like haltered horses, if blind, so much the quieter." The base of the new society was the freeman who fought, tilled, judged and grew from more to more. He wrought a state out of tribal kinship and fostered an independence and self-reliance which no oppression could destroy. The story of man's slow ascent from savagery through barbarism and self-mastery to civilization is the embodiment of the spirit of optimism. From the first hour of the new nations each century has seen a better Europe, until the development of the world demanded America.

Tolstoi said the other day that America, once the hope of the world, was in bondage to Mammon. Tolstoi and other Europeans have still much to learn about this great, free country of ours before they understand the unique civic struggle which America is undergoing. She is confronted with the mighty task of assimilating all the foreigners that are drawn together from every country, and welding them into one people with one national spirit. We have the right to demand the forbearance of critics until the United States has demonstrated whether she can make one people out of all the nations of the earth. London economists are alarmed at less than five hundred thousand foreign-born in a population of six million, and discuss earnestly the danger of too many aliens. But what is their problem in comparison with that of New York, which counts nearly one million five hundred thousand foreigners among its three and a half million citizens? Think of it! Every third person in our American metropolis is an alien. By these figures alone America's greatness can be measured.

It is true, America has devoted herself largely to the solution of material problems—breaking the fields, opening mines, irrigating deserts, spanning the continent with rail-roads; but she is doing these things in a new way, by educating her people, by placing at the service of every man's need every resource of human skill. She is transmuting her industrial wealth into the education of her workmen, so that unskilled people shall have no place in American life, so that all men shall bring mind and soul to the control of matter. Her children are not drudges and slaves. The Constitution has declared it, and the spirit of our institutions has confirmed it. The best the land can teach them they shall know. They shall learn that there is no upper class in their country, and no lower, and they shall understand how it is that God and His world are for everybody.

America might do all this, and still be selfish, still be a worshipper of Mammon. But America is the home of charity as well as of commerce. In the midst of roaring traffic, side by side with noisy factory and sky-reaching warehouse, one sees the school, the library, the hospital, the park—works of public benevolence which represent wealth wrought into ideas that shall endure forever. Behold what America has already done to alleviate suffering and restore the afflicted to society—given sight to the fingers of the blind, language to the dumb lip, and mind to the idiot clay, and tell me if indeed she worships Mammon only. Who shall measure the sympathy, skill and intelligence with which she ministers to all who come to her, and lessens the ever-swelling tide of poverty, misery and degradation which every year rolls against her gates from all the nations?

When I reflect on all these facts, I cannot but think that, Tolstoi and other theorists to the contrary, it is a splendid thing to be an American. In America the optimist finds abundant reason for confidence in the present and hope for the future, and this hope, this confidence, may well extend over all the great nations of the earth.

If we compare our own time with the past, we find in modern statistics a solid foundation for a confident and buoyant world-optimism. Beneath the doubt, the unrest, the materialism, which surround us still glows and burns at the world's best life a steadfast faith. To hear the pessimist, one would think civilization had bivouacked in the Middle Ages, and had not had marching orders since. He does not realize that the progress of evolution is not an uninterrupted march.

"Now touching goal, now backward hurl'd,
Toils the indomitable world."

I have recently read an address by one whose knowledge it would be presumptuous to challenge.[1] In it I find abundant evidence of progress.

During the past fifty years crime has decreased. True, the records of to-day contain a longer list of crime. But our statistics are more complete and accurate than the statistics of times past. Besides, there are many offences on the list which half a century ago would not have been thought of as crimes. This shows that the public conscience is more sensitive than it ever was.

Our definition of crime has grown stricter, our punishment of it more lenient and intelligent. The old feeling of revenge has largely disappeared. It is no longer an eye for an eye, a tooth for a tooth. The criminal is treated as one who is diseased. He is confined not merely for punishment, but because he is a menace to society. While he is under restraint, he is treated with humane care and disciplined so that his mind shall be cured of its disease, and he shall be restored to society able to do his part of its work.

Another sign of awakened and enlightened public conscience is the effort to provide the working-class with better houses. Did it occur to any one a hundred years ago to think whether the dwellings of the poor were sanitary, convenient or sunny? Do not forget that in the "good old times" cholera and typhus devastated whole counties, and that pestilence walked abroad in the capitals of Europe.

Not only have our laboring-classes better houses and better

---

[1] Address by the Hon. Carroll D. Wright before the Unitarian Conference, September, 1903.

places to work in; but employers recognize the right of the employed to seek more than the bare wage of existence. In the darkness and turmoil of our modern industrial strifes we discern but dimly the principles that underlie the struggle. The recognition of the right of all men to life, liberty and the pursuit of happiness, a spirit of conciliation such as Burke dreamed of, the willingness on the part of the strong to make concessions to the weak, the realization that the rights of the employer are bound up in the rights of the employed—in these the optimist beholds the signs of our times.

Another right which the State has recognized as belonging to each man is the right to an education. In the enlightened parts of Europe and in America every city, every town, every village, has its school; and it is no longer a class who have access to knowledge, for to the children of the poorest laborer the school-door stands open. From the civilized nations universal education is driving the dull host of illiteracy.

Education broadens to include all men, and deepens to reach all truths. Scholars are no longer confined to Greek, Latin and mathematics, but they also study science; and science converts the dreams of the poet, the theory of the mathematician and the fiction of the economist into ships, hospitals and instruments that enable one skilled hand to perform the work of a thousand. The student of to-day is not asked if he has learned his grammar. Is he a mere grammar-machine, a dry catalogue of scientific facts, or has he acquired the qualities of manliness? His supreme lesson is to grapple with great public questions, to keep his mind hospitable to new ideas and new views of truth, to restore the finer ideals that are lost sight of in the struggle for wealth and to promote justice between man and man. He learns that there may be substitutes for human labor—horse-power and machinery and books; but "there are no substitutes for common sense, patience, integrity, courage."

Who can doubt the vastness of the achievements of education when one considers how different the condition of the blind and the deaf is from what it was a century ago? They were then objects of superstitious pity, and shared the lowest beggar's lot. Everybody looked upon their case as hopeless, and this view plunged them deeper in despair. The blind themselves laughed in the face of Haüy when he offered to teach them to read. How pitiable is the cramped sense of imprisonment in circumstances which teaches men to expect no good and to treat any attempt to relieve them as the vagary of a disordered mind! But now, behold the transformation; see how institutions and industrial establishments for the blind have sprung up as if by magic; see how many of the deaf have learned not only to read and write, but to speak; and remember that the faith and patience of Dr. Howe have borne fruit in the efforts that are being made everywhere to educate the deaf-blind and equip them for the struggle. Do you wonder that I am full of hope and lifted up?

The highest result of education is tolerance. Long ago men fought and died for their faith; but it took ages to teach them the other kind of courage,—the courage to recognize the faiths of their brethren and their rights of conscience. Tolerance is the first principle of community; it is the spirit which conserves the best that all men think. No loss by flood and lightning, no destruction of cities and temples by the hostile forces of nature, has deprived man of so many noble lives and impulses as those which his intolerance has destroyed.

With wonder and sorrow I go back in thought to the ages of intolerance and bigotry. I see Jesus received with scorn and nailed on the cross. I see his followers hounded and tortured and burned. I am present where the finer spirits that revolt from the superstition of the Middle Ages are accused of impiety and stricken down. I behold the children of Israel reviled and per-secuted unto death by those who pretend Christianity with the tongue; I see them driven from land to land, hunted from refuge to refuge, summoned to the felon's place, exposed to the whip, mocked as they utter amid the pain of martyrdom a confession of the faith which they have kept with such splendid constancy. The same bigotry that oppresses the Jews falls tiger-like upon Christian nonconformists of purest lives and wipes out the Albigenses and the peaceful Vaudois, "whose bones lie on the mountains cold." I see the clouds part slowly, and I hear a cry of protest against the bigot. The restraining hand of tolerance is laid upon the inquisitor, and the humanist utters a message of peace to the persecuted. Instead of the cry, "Burn the heretic!" men study the human soul with sympathy, and there enters into their hearts a new reverence for that which is unseen.

The idea of brotherhood redawns upon the world with a broader significance than the narrow association of members in a sect or creed; and thinkers of great soul like Lessing challenge the world to say which is more godlike, the hatred and tooth-and-nail grapple of conflicting religions, or sweet accord and mutual helpfulness. Ancient prejudice of man against his brotherman wavers and retreats before the radiance of a more generous sentiment, which will not sacrifice men to forms, or rob them of the comfort and strength they find in their own beliefs. The heresy of one age becomes the orthodoxy of the next. Mere tolerance has given place to a sentiment of brotherhood between sincere men of all denominations. The optimist rejoices in the affectionate sympathy between Catholic heart and Protestant heart which finds a gratifying expression in the universal respect and warm admiration for Leo XIII on the part of good men the world over. The centenary celebrations of the births of Emerson and Channing are beautiful examples of the tribute which men of all creeds pay to the memory of a pure soul.

Thus in my outlook upon our times I find that I am glad to be a citizen of the world, and as I regard my country, I find that to be an American is to be an optimist. I know the unhappy and unrighteous story of what has been done in the Philippines beneath our flag; but I believe that in the accidents of statecraft the best intelligence of the people sometimes fails to express itself. I read in the history of Julius Cæsar that during the civil wars there were millions of peaceful herdsmen and laborers who worked as long as they could, and fled before the advance of the armies that were led by the few, then waited until the danger was past, and returned to repair damages with patient hands. So the people are patient and honest, while their rulers stumble. I rejoice to see in the world and in this country a new and better patriotism than that which seeks the life of an enemy. It is a patriotism higher than that of the battle-field. It moves thousands to lay down their lives in social service, and every life so laid down brings us a step nearer the time when corn-fields shall no more be fields of battle. So when I heard of the cruel fighting in the Philippines, I did not despair, because I knew that the hearts of our people were not in that fight, and that sometime the hand of the destroyer must be stayed.

Part III. The Practice of Optimism

THE test of all beliefs is their practical effect in life. If it be true that optimism compels the world forward, and pessimism retards it, then it is dangerous to propagate a pessimistic philosophy. One who believes that the pain in the world outweighs the joy, and expresses that unhappy conviction, only adds to the pain. Schopenhauer is an enemy to the race. Even if he earnestly believed that this is the most wretched of possible worlds, he should not promulgate a doctrine which robs men of the incentive to fight with circumstance. If Life gave him ashes for bread, it was his fault. Life is a fair field, and the right will prosper if we stand by our guns.

Let pessimism once take hold of the mind, and life is all topsy-turvy, all vanity and vexation of spirit. There is no cure for individual or social disorder, except in forgetfulness and annihilation. "Let us eat, drink and be merry," says the pessimist, "for to-morrow we die." If I regarded my life from the point of view of the pessimist, I should be undone. I should seek in vain for the light that does not visit my eyes and the music that does not ring in my ears. I should beg night and day and never be satisfied. I should sit apart in awful solitude, a prey to fear and despair. But since I consider it a duty to myself and to others to be happy, I escape a misery worse than any physical deprivation.

Who shall dare let his incapacity for hope or goodness cast a shadow upon the courage of those who bear their burdens as if they were privileges? The optimist cannot fall back, cannot falter; for he knows his neighbor will be hindered by his failure to keep in line. He will therefore hold his place fearlessly and remember the duty of silence. Sufficient unto each heart is its own sorrow. He will take the iron claws of circumstance in his hand and use them as tools to break away the obstacles that block his path. He will work as if upon him alone depended the establishment of heaven on earth.

We have seen that the world's philosophers—the Sayers of the Word were—optimists; so also are the men of action and achievement—the Doers of the Word. Dr. Howe found his way to Laura Bridgman's soul because he began with the belief that he could reach it. English jurists had said that the deaf-blind were idiots in the eyes of the law. Behold what the optimist does. He controverts a hard legal axiom; he looks behind the dull impassive clay and sees a human soul in bondage, and quietly, resolutely sets about its deliverance. His efforts are victorious. He creates intelligence out of idiocy and proves to the law that the deaf-blind man is a responsible being.

When Haüy offered to teach the blind to read, he was met by pessimism that laughed at his folly. Had he not believed that the soul of man is mightier than the ignorance that fetters it, had he not been an optimist, he would not have turned the fingers of the blind into new instruments. No pessimist ever discovered the secrets of the stars, or sailed to an uncharted land, or opened a new heaven to the human spirit. St. Bernard was so deeply an optimist that he believed two hundred and fifty enlightened men could illuminate the darkness which overwhelmed the period of the Crusades; and the light of his faith broke like a new day upon western Europe. John Bosco, the benefactor of the poor and the friendless of Italian cities, was another optimist, another prophet who, perceiving a Divine Idea while it was yet afar, proclaimed it to his countrymen. Although they laughed at his vision and called him a madman, yet he worked on patiently, and with the labor of his hands he maintained a home for little street waifs. In the fervor of enthusiasm he predicted the wonderful movement which should result from his work. Even in the days before he had money or patronage, he drew glowing pictures of the splendid system of schools and hospitals which should spread from one end of Italy to the other, and he lived to see the organization of the San Salvador Society, which was the embodiment of his prophetic optimism. When

Dr. Seguin declared his opinion that the feeble-minded could be taught, again people laughed, and in their complacent wisdom said he was no better than an idiot himself. But the noble optimist persevered, and by and by the reluctant pessimists saw that he whom they ridiculed had become one of the world's philanthropists. Thus the optimist believes, attempts, achieves. He stands always in the sunlight. Some day the wonderful, the inexpressible, arrives and shines upon him, and he is there to welcome it. His soul meets his own and beats a glad march to every new discovery, every fresh victory over difficulties, every addition to human knowledge and happiness.

We have found that our great philosophers and our great men of action are optimists. So, too, our most potent men of letters have been optimists in their books and in their lives. No pessimist ever won an audience commensurately wide with his genius, and many optimistic writers have been read and admired out of all measure to their talents, simply because they wrote of the sunlit side of life. Dickens, Lamb, Goldsmith, Irving, all the well-beloved and gentle humorists, were optimists. Swift, the pessimist, has never had as many readers as his towering genius should command, and indeed, when he comes down into our century and meets Thackeray, that generous optimist can hardly do him justice. In spite of the latter-day notoriety of the "Rubái-yát" of Omar Khayyám, we may set it down as a rule that he who would be heard must be a believer, must have a fundamental optimism in his philosophy. He may bluster and disagree and lament as Carlyle and Ruskin do sometimes; but a basic confidence in the good destiny of life and of the world must underlie his work.

Shakespeare is the prince of optimists. His tragedies are a revelation of moral order. In "Lear" and "Hamlet" there is a looking forward to something better, some one is left at the end of the play to right wrong, restore society and build the state anew. The later plays, "The Tempest" and "Cymbeline," show a beautiful, placid optimism which delights in reconciliations and reunions and which plans for the triumph of external as well as internal good.

If Browning were less difficult to read, he would surely be

the dominant poet in this century. I feel the ecstasy with which he exclaims, "Oh, good gigantic smile o' the brown old earth this autumn morning!" And how he sets my brain going when he says, because there is imperfection, there must be perfection; completeness must come of incompleteness; failure is an evidence of triumph for the fulness of the days. Yes, discord is, that harmony may be; pain destroys, that health may renew; perhaps I am deaf and blind that others likewise afflicted may see and hear with a more perfect sense! From Browning I learn that there is no lost good, and that makes it easier for me to go at life, right or wrong, do the best I know, and fear not. My heart responds proudly to his exhortation to pay gladly life's debt of pain, darkness and cold. Lift up your burden, it is God's gift, bear it nobly.

The man of letters whose voice is to prevail must be an optimist, and his voice often learns its message from his life. Stevenson's life has become a tradition only ten years after his death; he has taken his place among the heroes, the bravest man of letters since Johnson and Lamb. I remember an hour when I was discouraged and ready to falter. For days I had been pegging away at a task which refused to get itself accomplished. In the midst of my perplexity I read an essay of Stevenson which made me feel as if I had been "outing" in the sunshine, instead of losing heart over a difficult task. I tried again with new courage and succeeded almost before I knew it. I have failed many times since; but I have never felt so disheartened as I did before that sturdy preacher gave me my lesson in the "fashion of the smiling face."

Read Schopenhauer and Omar, and you will grow to find the world as hollow as they find it. Read Green's history of England, and the world is peopled with heroes. I never knew why Green's history thrilled me with the vigor of romance until I read his biography. Then I learned how his quick imagination transfigured the hard, bare facts of life into new and living dreams. When he and his wife were too poor to have a fire, he would sit before the unlit hearth and pretend that it was ablaze. "Drill your thoughts," he said; "shut out the gloomy and call in the bright. There is more wisdom in shutting one's eyes than your copybook philosophers will allow."

Every optimist moves along with progress and hastens it, while every pessimist would keep the world at a standstill. The consequence of pessimism in the life of a nation is the same as in the life of the individual. Pessimism kills the instinct that urges men to struggle against poverty, ignorance and crime, and dries up all the fountains of joy in the world. In imagination I leave the country which lifts up the manhood of the poor and I visit India, the underworld of fatalism—where three hundred million human beings, scarcely men, submerged in ignorance and misery, precipitate themselves still deeper into the pit. Why are they thus? Because they have for thousands of years been the victims of their philosophy, which teaches them that men are as grass, and the grass fadeth, and there is no more greenness upon the earth. They sit in the shadow and let the circumstances they should master grip them, until they cease to be Men, and are made to dance and salaam like puppets in a play. After a little hour death comes and hurries them off to the grave, and other puppets with other "pasteboard passions and desires" take their place, and the show goes on for centuries.

Go to India and see what sort of civilization is developed when a nation lacks faith in progress and bows to the gods of darkness. Under the influence of Brahminism genius and ambition have been suppressed. There is no one to befriend the poor or to protect the fatherless and the widow. The sick lie untended. The blind know not how to see, nor the deaf to hear, and they are left by the roadside to die. In India it is a sin to teach the blind and the deaf because their affliction is regarded as a punishment for offences in a previous state of existence. If I had been born in the midst of these fatalistic doctrines, I should still be in darkness, my life a desert-land where no caravan of thought might pass between my spirit and the world beyond.

The Hindoos believe in endurance, but not in resistance; therefore they have been subdued by strangers. Their history is a repetition of that of Babylon. A nation from afar came with speed swiftly, and none stumbled, or slept, or slumbered, but they brought desolation upon the land, and took the stay and the staff from the people, the whole stay of bread, and the whole stay of water, the mighty man, and the man of war, the judge, and the prophet, and the prudent, and the ancient, and none delivered them. Woe, indeed, is the heritage of those who walk sad-thoughted and downcast through this radiant, soul-delighting earth, blind to its beauty and deaf to its music, and of those who call evil good, and good evil, and put darkness for light, and light for darkness.

What care the weather-bronzed sons of the West, feeding the world from the plains of Dakota, for the Omars and the Brahmins? They would say to the Hindoos, "Blot out your philosophy, dead for a thousand years, look with fresh eyes at Reality and Life, put away your Brahmins and your crooked gods, and seek diligently for Vishnu the Preserver."

Optimism is the faith that leads to achievement; nothing can be done without hope. When our forefathers laid the foundation of the American commonwealths, what nerved them to their task but a vision of a free community? Against the cold, inhospitable sky, across the wilderness white with snow, where lurked the hidden savage, gleamed the bow of promise, toward which they set their faces with the faith that levels mountains, fills up valleys, bridges rivers and carries civilization to the uttermost parts of the earth. Although the pioneers could not build according to the Hebraic ideal they saw, yet they gave the pattern of all that is most enduring in our country to-day. They brought to the wilderness the thinking mind, the printed book, the deep-rooted desire for self-government and the English common law that judges alike the king and the subject, the law on which rests the whole structure of our society.

It is significant that the foundation of that law is optimistic. In Latin countries the court proceeds with a pessimistic bias. The prisoner is held guilty until he is proved innocent. In England and the United States there is an optimistic presumption that the accused is innocent until it is no longer possible to deny his guilt. Under our system, it is said, many criminals are acquitted; but it is surely better so than that many innocent persons should suffer. The pessimist cries, "There is no enduring good in man! The tendency of all things is through perpetual loss to chaos in the end. If there was ever an idea of good in things evil, it was impotent, and the world rushes on to ruin." But behold, the law of the two most sober-minded, practical and law-abiding nations on earth assumes the good in man and demands a proof of the bad.

Optimism is the faith that leads to achievement. The prophets of the world have been of good heart, or their standards would have stood naked in the field without a defender. Tolstoi's strictures lose power because they are pessimistic. If he had seen clearly the faults of America, and still believed in her capacity to overcome them, our people might have felt the stimulation of his censure. But the world turns its back on a hopeless prophet and listens to Emerson who takes into account the best qualities of the nation and attacks only the vices which no one can defend or deny. It listens to the strong man, Lincoln, who in times of doubt, trouble and need does not falter. He sees success afar, and by strenuous hope, by hoping against hope, inspires a nation. Through the night of despair he says, "All is well," and thousands rest in his confidence. When such a man censures, and points to a fault, the nation obeys, and his words sink into the ears of men; but to the lamentations of the habitual Jeremiah the ear grows dull.

Our newspapers should remember this. The press is the pulpit of the modern world, and on the preachers who fill it much depends. If the protest of the press against unrighteous measures is to avail, then for ninety-nine days the word of the preacher should be buoyant and of good cheer, so that on the hundredth day the voice of censure may be a hundred times strong. This was Lincoln's way. He knew the people; he believed in them and rested his faith on the justice and wisdom of the great majority. When in his rough and ready way he said, "You can't fool all the people all the time," he expressed a great principle, the doctrine of faith in human nature.

The prophet is not without honor, save he be a pessimist. The ecstatic prophecies of Isaiah did far more to restore the exiles of Israel to their homes than the lamentations of Jeremiah did to deliver them from the hands of evil-doers.

Even on Christmas Day do men remember that Christ came as a prophet of good? His joyous optimism is like water to feverish lips, and has for its highest expression the eight beatitudes. It is because Christ is an optimist that for ages he has dominated the Western world. For nineteen centuries Christendom has gazed into his shining face and felt that all things work together for good. St. Paul, too, taught the faith which looks beyond the hardest things into the infinite horizon of heaven, where all limitations are lost in the light of perfect understanding. If you are born blind, search the treasures of darkness. They are more precious than the gold of Ophir. They are love and goodness and truth and hope, and their price is above rubies and sapphires.

Jesus utters and Paul proclaims a message of peace and a message of reason, a belief in the Idea, not in things, in love, not in conquest. The optimist is he who sees that men's actions are directed not by squadrons and armies, but by moral power, that the conquests of Alexander and Napoleon are less abiding than Newton's and Galileo's and St. Augustine's silent mastery of the world. Ideas are mightier than fire and sword. Noiselessly they propagate themselves from land to land, and mankind goes out and reaps the rich harvest and thanks God; but the achievements of the warrior are like his canvas city, "to-day a camp, to-morrow all struck and vanished, a few pit-holes and heaps of straw." This was the gospel of Jesus two thousand years ago. Christmas Day is the festival of optimism.

Although there are still great evils which have not been subdued, and the optimist is not blind to them, yet he is full of hope. Despondency has no place in his creed, for he believes in the imperishable righteousness of God and the dignity of man. History records man's triumphant ascent. Each halt in his progress has been but a pause before a mighty leap forward. The time is not out of joint. If indeed some of the temples we worshipped in have fallen, we have built new ones on the sacred sites loftier and holier than those which have crumbled. If we have lost some of the heroic physical qualities of our ancestors, we have replaced them with a spiritual nobleness that turns aside wrath and binds up the wounds of the vanquished. All the past attainments of man are ours; and more, his day-dreams have become our clear realities. Therein lies our hope and sure faith.

As I stand in the sunshine of a sincere and earnest optimism, my imagination "paints yet more glorious triumphs on the cloud-curtain of the future." Out of the fierce struggle and turmoil of contending systems and powers I see a brighter spiritual era slowly emerge—an era in which there shall be no England, no France, no Germany, no America, no this people or that, but one family, the human race; one law, peace; one need, harmony; one means, labor; one taskmaster, God.

If I should try to say anew the creed of the optimist, I should say something like this: "I believe in God, I believe in man, I believe in the power of the spirit. I believe it is a sacred duty to encourage ourselves and others; to hold the tongue from any unhappy word against God's world, because no man has any right to complain of a universe which God made good, and which thousands of men have striven to keep good. I believe we should so act that we may draw nearer and more near the age when no man shall live at his ease while another suffers." These are the articles of my faith, and there is yet another on which all depends—to bear this faith above every tempest which overfloods it, and to make it a principle in disaster and through affliction. Optimism is the harmony between man's spirit and the spirit of God pronouncing His works good.

A CATALOG OF SELECTED
DOVER BOOKS
IN ALL FIELDS OF INTEREST

A CATALOG OF SELECTED DOVER
BOOKS IN ALL FIELDS OF INTEREST

CONCERNING THE SPIRITUAL IN ART, Wassily Kandinsky. Pioneering work by father of abstract art. Thoughts on color theory, nature of art. Analysis of earlier masters. 12 illustrations. 80pp. of text. 5⅜ x 8½. 0-486-23411-8

CELTIC ART: The Methods of Construction, George Bain. Simple geometric techniques for making Celtic interlacements, spirals, Kells-type initials, animals, humans, etc. Over 500 illustrations. 160pp. 9 x 12. (Available in U.S. only.) 0-486-22923-8

AN ATLAS OF ANATOMY FOR ARTISTS, Fritz Schider. Most thorough reference work on art anatomy in the world. Hundreds of illustrations, including selections from works by Vesalius, Leonardo, Goya, Ingres, Michelangelo, others. 593 illustrations. 192pp. 7⅛ x 10¼. 0-486-20241-0

CELTIC HAND STROKE-BY-STROKE (Irish Half-Uncial from "The Book of Kells"): An Arthur Baker Calligraphy Manual, Arthur Baker. Complete guide to creating each letter of the alphabet in distinctive Celtic manner. Covers hand position, strokes, pens, inks, paper, more. Illustrated. 48pp. 8¼ x 11. 0-486-24336-2

EASY ORIGAMI, John Montroll. Charming collection of 32 projects (hat, cup, pelican, piano, swan, many more) specially designed for the novice origami hobbyist. Clearly illustrated easy-to-follow instructions insure that even beginning papercrafters will achieve successful results. 48pp. 8¼ x 11. 0-486-27298-2

BLOOMINGDALE'S ILLUSTRATED 1886 CATALOG: Fashions, Dry Goods and Housewares, Bloomingdale Brothers. Famed merchants' extremely rare catalog depicting about 1,700 products: clothing, housewares, firearms, dry goods, jewelry, more. Invaluable for dating, identifying vintage items. Also, copyright-free graphics for artists, designers. Co-published with Henry Ford Museum & Greenfield Village. 160pp. 8¼ x 11. 0-486-25780-0

THE ART OF WORLDLY WISDOM, Baltasar Gracian. "Think with the few and speak with the many," "Friends are a second existence," and "Be able to forget" are among this 1637 volume's 300 pithy maxims. A perfect source of mental and spiritual refreshment, it can be opened at random and appreciated either in brief or at length. 128pp. 5⅜ x 8½. 0-486-44034-6

JOHNSON'S DICTIONARY: A Modern Selection, Samuel Johnson (E. L. McAdam and George Milne, eds.). This modern version reduces the original 1755 edition's 2,300 pages of definitions and literary examples to a more manageable length, retaining the verbal pleasure and historical curiosity of the original. 480pp. 5⁹⁄₁₆ x 8¼. 0-486-44089-3

ADVENTURES OF HUCKLEBERRY FINN, Mark Twain, Illustrated by E. W. Kemble. A work of eternal richness and complexity, a source of ongoing critical debate, and a literary landmark, Twain's 1885 masterpiece about a barefoot boy's journey of self-discovery has enthralled readers around the world. This handsome clothbound reproduction of the first edition features all 174 of the original black-and-white illustrations. 368pp. 5⅜ x 8½. 0-486-44322-1

STICKLEY CRAFTSMAN FURNITURE CATALOGS, Gustav Stickley and L. & J. G. Stickley. Beautiful, functional furniture in two authentic catalogs from 1910. 594 illustrations, including 277 photos, show settles, rockers, armchairs, reclining chairs, bookcases, desks, tables. 183pp. 6½ x 9¼. 0-486-23838-5

AMERICAN LOCOMOTIVES IN HISTORIC PHOTOGRAPHS: 1858 to 1949, Ron Ziel (ed.). A rare collection of 126 meticulously detailed official photographs, called "builder portraits," of American locomotives that majestically chronicle the rise of steam locomotive power in America. Introduction. Detailed captions. xi+ 129pp. 9 x 12.
0-486-27393-8

AMERICA'S LIGHTHOUSES: An Illustrated History, Francis Ross Holland, Jr. Delightfully written, profusely illustrated fact-filled survey of over 200 American lighthouses since 1716. History, anecdotes, technological advances, more. 240pp. 8 x 10¾. 0-486-25576-X

TOWARDS A NEW ARCHITECTURE, Le Corbusier. Pioneering manifesto by founder of "International School." Technical and aesthetic theories, views of industry, economics, relation of form to function, "mass-production split" and much more. Profusely illustrated. 320pp. 6⅛ x 9¼. (Available in U.S. only.) 0-486-25023-7

HOW THE OTHER HALF LIVES, Jacob Riis. Famous journalistic record, exposing poverty and degradation of New York slums around 1900, by major social reformer. 100 striking and influential photographs. 233pp. 10 x 7⅞. 0-486-22012-5

FRUIT KEY AND TWIG KEY TO TREES AND SHRUBS, William M. Harlow. One of the handiest and most widely used identification aids. Fruit key covers 120 deciduous and evergreen species; twig key 160 deciduous species. Easily used. Over 300 photographs. 126pp. 5⅜ x 8½. 0-486-20511-8

COMMON BIRD SONGS, Dr. Donald J. Borror. Songs of 60 most common U.S. birds: robins, sparrows, cardinals, bluejays, finches, more—arranged in order of increasing complexity. Up to 9 variations of songs of each species.
Cassette and manual 0-486-99911-4

ORCHIDS AS HOUSE PLANTS, Rebecca Tyson Northen. Grow cattleyas and many other kinds of orchids—in a window, in a case, or under artificial light. 63 illustrations. 148pp. 5⅜ x 8½. 0-486-23261-1

MONSTER MAZES, Dave Phillips. Masterful mazes at four levels of difficulty. Avoid deadly perils and evil creatures to find magical treasures. Solutions for all 32 exciting illustrated puzzles. 48pp. 8¼ x 11. 0-486-26005-4

MOZART'S DON GIOVANNI (DOVER OPERA LIBRETTO SERIES), Wolfgang Amadeus Mozart. Introduced and translated by Ellen H. Bleiler. Standard Italian libretto, with complete English translation. Convenient and thoroughly portable—an ideal companion for reading along with a recording or the performance itself. Introduction. List of characters. Plot summary. 121pp. 5¼ x 8½. 0-486-24944-1

FRANK LLOYD WRIGHT'S DANA HOUSE, Donald Hoffmann. Pictorial essay of residential masterpiece with over 160 interior and exterior photos, plans, elevations, sketches and studies. 128pp. 9¼ x 10¾. 0-486-29120-0

FRENCH STORIES/CONTES FRANÇAIS: A Dual-Language Book, Wallace Fowlie. Ten stories by French masters, Voltaire to Camus: "Micromegas" by Voltaire; "The Atheist's Mass" by Balzac; "Minuet" by de Maupassant; "The Guest" by Camus, six more. Excellent English translations on facing pages. Also French-English vocabulary list, exercises, more. 352pp. 5⅜ x 8½. 0-486-26443-2

CHICAGO AT THE TURN OF THE CENTURY IN PHOTOGRAPHS: 122 Historic Views from the Collections of the Chicago Historical Society, Larry A. Viskochil. Rare large-format prints offer detailed views of City Hall, State Street, the Loop, Hull House, Union Station, many other landmarks, circa 1904-1913. Introduction. Captions. Maps. 144pp. 9⅜ x 12¼. 0-486-24656-6

OLD BROOKLYN IN EARLY PHOTOGRAPHS, 1865–1929, William Lee Younger. Luna Park, Gravesend race track, construction of Grand Army Plaza, moving of Hotel Brighton, etc. 157 previously unpublished photographs. 165pp. 8⅞ x 11¾.

0-486-23587-4

THE MYTHS OF THE NORTH AMERICAN INDIANS, Lewis Spence. Rich anthology of the myths and legends of the Algonquins, Iroquois, Pawnees and Sioux, prefaced by an extensive historical and ethnological commentary. 36 illustrations. 480pp. 5⅜ x 8½. 0-486-25967-6

AN ENCYCLOPEDIA OF BATTLES: Accounts of Over 1,560 Battles from 1479 B.C. to the Present, David Eggenberger. Essential details of every major battle in recorded history from the first battle of Megiddo in 1479 B.C. to Grenada in 1984. List of Battle Maps. New Appendix covering the years 1967–1984. Index. 99 illustrations. 544pp. 6½ x 9¼. 0-486-24913-1

SAILING ALONE AROUND THE WORLD, Captain Joshua Slocum. First man to sail around the world, alone, in small boat. One of the great feats of seamanship told in delightful manner. 67 illustrations. 294pp. 5⅜ x 8½. 0-486-20326-3

ANARCHISM AND OTHER ESSAYS, Emma Goldman. Powerful, penetrating, prophetic essays on direct action, role of minorities, prison reform, puritan hypocrisy, violence, etc. 271pp. 5⅜ x 8½. 0-486-22484-8

MYTHS OF THE HINDUS AND BUDDHISTS, Ananda K. Coomaraswamy and Sister Nivedita. Great stories of the epics; deeds of Krishna, Shiva, taken from puranas, Vedas, folk tales; etc. 32 illustrations. 400pp. 5⅜ x 8½. 0-486-21759-0

MY BONDAGE AND MY FREEDOM, Frederick Douglass. Born a slave, Douglass became outspoken force in antislavery movement. The best of Douglass' autobiographies. Graphic description of slave life. 464pp. 5⅜ x 8½. 0-486-22457-0

FOLLOWING THE EQUATOR: A Journey Around the World, Mark Twain. Fascinating humorous account of 1897 voyage to Hawaii, Australia, India, New Zealand, etc. Ironic, bemused reports on peoples, customs, climate, flora and fauna, politics, much more. 197 illustrations. 720pp. 5⅜ x 8½. 0-486-26113-1

GREAT SPEECHES BY AMERICAN WOMEN, edited by James Daley. Here are 21 legendary speeches from the country's most inspirational female voices, including Sojourner Truth, Susan B. Anthony, Eleanor Roosevelt, Hillary Rodham Clinton, Nancy Pelosi, and many others. 192pp. 5³⁄₁₆ x 8¼. 0-486-46141-6

THE MYTHS OF GREECE AND ROME, H. A. Guerber. A classic of mythology, generously illustrated, long prized for its simple, graphic, accurate retelling of the principal myths of Greece and Rome, and for its commentary on their origins and significance. With 64 illustrations by Michelangelo, Raphael, Titian, Rubens, Canova, Bernini and others. 480pp. 5⅜ x 8½. 0-486-27584-1

PSYCHOLOGY OF MUSIC, Carl E. Seashore. Classic work discusses music as a medium from psychological viewpoint. Clear treatment of physical acoustics, auditory apparatus, sound perception, development of musical skills, nature of musical feeling, host of other topics. 88 figures. 408pp. 5⅜ x 8½.   0-486-21851-1

LIFE IN ANCIENT EGYPT, Adolf Erman. Fullest, most thorough, detailed older account with much not in more recent books, domestic life, religion, magic, medicine, commerce, much more. Many illustrations reproduce tomb paintings, carvings, hieroglyphs, etc. 597pp. 5⅜ x 8½.   0-486-22632-8

SUNDIALS, Their Theory and Construction, Albert Waugh. Far and away the best, most thorough coverage of ideas, mathematics concerned, types, construction, adjusting anywhere. Simple, nontechnical treatment allows even children to build several of these dials. Over 100 illustrations. 230pp. 5⅜ x 8½.   0-486-22947-5

GREAT SPEECHES BY AFRICAN AMERICANS: Frederick Douglass, Sojourner Truth, Dr. Martin Luther King, Jr., Barack Obama, and Others, edited by James Daley. Tracing the struggle for freedom and civil rights across two centuries, this anthology comprises speeches by Martin Luther King, Jr., Marcus Garvey, Malcolm X, Barack Obama, and many other influential figures. 160pp. 5³⁄₁₆ x 8¼.   0-486-44761-8

OLD-TIME VIGNETTES IN FULL COLOR, Carol Belanger Grafton (ed.). Over 390 charming, often sentimental illustrations, selected from archives of Victorian graphics—pretty women posing, children playing, food, flowers, kittens and puppies, smiling cherubs, birds and butterflies, much more. All copyright-free. 48pp. 9¼ x 12¼.
                    0-486-27269-9

PERSPECTIVE FOR ARTISTS, Rex Vicat Cole. Depth, perspective of sky and sea, shadows, much more, not usually covered. 391 diagrams, 81 reproductions of drawings and paintings. 279pp. 5⅜ x 8½.   0-486-22487-2

DRAWING THE LIVING FIGURE, Joseph Sheppard. Innovative approach to artistic anatomy focuses on specifics of surface anatomy, rather than muscles and bones. Over 170 drawings of live models in front, back and side views, and in widely varying poses. Accompanying diagrams. 177 illustrations. Introduction. Index. 144pp. 8⅜ x11¼.
                    0-486-26723-7

GOTHIC AND OLD ENGLISH ALPHABETS: 100 Complete Fonts, Dan X. Solo. Add power, elegance to posters, signs, other graphics with 100 stunning copyright- free alphabets: Blackstone, Dolbey, Germania, 97 more—including many lower-case, numerals, punctuation marks. 104pp. 8⅛ x 11.   0-486-24695-7

THE BOOK OF WOOD CARVING, Charles Marshall Sayers. Finest book for beginners discusses fundamentals and offers 34 designs. "Absolutely first rate . . . well thought out and well executed."–E. J. Tangerman. 118pp. 7¾ x 10⅝.   0-486-23654-4

ILLUSTRATED CATALOG OF CIVIL WAR MILITARY GOODS: Union Army Weapons, Insignia, Uniform Accessories, and Other Equipment, Schuyler, Hartley, and Graham. Rare, profusely illustrated 1846 catalog includes Union Army uniform and dress regulations, arms and ammunition, coats, insignia, flags, swords, rifles, etc. 226 illustrations. 160pp. 9 x 12.   0-486-24939-5

WOMEN'S FASHIONS OF THE EARLY 1900s: An Unabridged Republication of "New York Fashions, 1909," National Cloak & Suit Co. Rare catalog of mail-order fashions documents women's and children's clothing styles shortly after the turn of the century. Captions offer full descriptions, prices. Invaluable resource for fashion, costume historians. Approximately 725 illustrations. 128pp. 8⅜ x 11¼.   0-486-27276-1

CATALOG OF DOVER BOOKS

LIGHT AND SHADE: A Classic Approach to Three-Dimensional Drawing, Mrs. Mary P. Merrifield. Handy reference clearly demonstrates principles of light and shade by revealing effects of common daylight, sunshine, and candle or artificial light on geometrical solids. 13 plates. 64pp. 5⅜ x 8½. 0-486-44143-1

ASTROLOGY AND ASTRONOMY: A Pictorial Archive of Signs and Symbols, Ernst and Johanna Lehner. Treasure trove of stories, lore, and myth, accompanied by more than 300 rare illustrations of planets, the Milky Way, signs of the zodiac, comets, meteors, and other astronomical phenomena. 192pp. 8⅜ x 11. 0-486-43981-X

JEWELRY MAKING: Techniques for Metal, Tim McCreight. Easy-to-follow instructions and carefully executed illustrations describe tools and techniques, use of gems and enamels, wire inlay, casting, and other topics. 72 line illustrations and diagrams. 176pp. 8¼ x 10⅞. 0-486-44043-5

MAKING BIRDHOUSES: Easy and Advanced Projects, Gladstone Califf. Easy-to-follow instructions include diagrams for everything from a one-room house for bluebirds to a forty-two-room structure for purple martins. 56 plates; 4 figures. 80pp. 8¾ x 6⅜. 0-486-44183-0

LITTLE BOOK OF LOG CABINS: How to Build and Furnish Them, William S. Wicks. Handy how-to manual, with instructions and illustrations for building cabins in the Adirondack style, fireplaces, stairways, furniture, beamed ceilings, and more. 102 line drawings. 96pp. 8¾ x 6⅜. 0-486-44259-4

THE SEASONS OF AMERICA PAST, Eric Sloane. From "sugaring time" and strawberry picking to Indian summer and fall harvest, a whole year's activities described in charming prose and enhanced with 79 of the author's own illustrations. 160pp. 8¼ x 11. 0-486-44220-9

THE METROPOLIS OF TOMORROW, Hugh Ferriss. Generous, prophetic vision of the metropolis of the future, as perceived in 1929. Powerful illustrations of towering structures, wide avenues, and rooftop parks—all features in many of today's modern cities. 59 illustrations. 144pp. 8¼ x 11. 0-486-43727-2

THE PATH TO ROME, Hilaire Belloc. This 1902 memoir abounds in lively vignettes from a vanished time, recounting a pilgrimage on foot across the Alps and Apennines in order to "see all Europe which the Christian Faith has saved." 77 of the author's original line drawings complement his sparkling prose. 272pp. 5⅜ x 8½. 0-486-44001-X

THE HISTORY OF RASSELAS: Prince of Abissinia, Samuel Johnson. Distinguished English writer attacks eighteenth-century optimism and man's unrealistic estimates of what life has to offer. 112pp. 5⅜ x 8½. 0-486-44094-X

A VOYAGE TO ARCTURUS, David Lindsay. A brilliant flight of pure fancy, where wild creatures crowd the fantastic landscape and demented torturers dominate victims with their bizarre mental powers. 272pp. 5⅜ x 8½. 0-486-44198-9

Paperbound unless otherwise indicated. Available at your book dealer, online at **www.doverpublications.com**, or by writing to Dept. GI, Dover Publications, Inc., 31 East 2nd Street, Mineola, NY 11501. For current price information or for free catalogs (please indicate field of interest), write to Dover Publications or log on to **www.doverpublications.com** and see every Dover book in print. Dover publishes more than 400 books each year on science, elementary and advanced mathematics, biology, music, art, literary history, social sciences, and other areas.